P9-DJL-709

THE ENTREPRENEURIAL AUTHOR™

{ *Achieving Success and Balance as a Writer in the 21st Century* }

Jay Conrad Levinson
and David L. Hancock

WILLIAMSBURG REGIONAL LIBRARY
7770 CROAKER ROAD
WILLIAMSBURG, VIRGINIA 23188

APR - - 2012

NEW YORK

{ The Entrepreneurial AUTHOR™ *Jay Conrad Levinson and David L. Hancock* }

Copyright © 2010 Jay Conrad Levinson and David L. Hancock

No part of this publication may be reproduced or transmitted in any form or by any means, mechanical or electronic, including photocopying and recording, or by any information storage and retrieval system, without permission in writing from author or publisher (except by a reviewer, who may quote brief passages and/or show brief video clips in review).

ISBN: 978-1-93359-686-0 (Paperback)
Library of Congress Control Number: 2009909626

Published by:

www.morganjamespublishing.com

Morgan James Publishing
1225 Franklin Ave Ste 325
Garden City, NY 11530-1693
Toll Free 800-485-4943
www.MorganJamesPublishing.com

Cover/Interior Design by:
Rachel Lopez
rachel@r2cdesign.com

In an effort to support local communities, raise awareness and funds, Morgan James Publishing donates one percent of all book sales for the life of each book to Habitat for Humanity. Get involved today, visit **www.HelpHabitatForHumanity.org.**

{Dedication}

Dedicated to those who use it.

{Table of Contents}

{FOREWORD}

We all know the scene from *The Wizard of Oz*. Dorothy and her motley bunch of friends finally make it to the Emerald City in the enchanted Land of Oz. They have survived attacks from angry apple trees, a field full of narcotic poppies, and their own bouts of self-doubt. They have made it to the Promised Land, but the little green guy at the door with his shifty eyes and bushy eyebrows bars their way into the place they have fought so hard to get to. But he relents and lets them in because Dorothy has something he wants—the ruby slippers. They're magical; they're powerful. They protect people from bad witches, and they hold the key to Dorothy's success.

Almost everyone in the world wants to write a book. Really. Eighty percent of the population thinks they have something important to say. And you know what? Everyone should be an author, especially if you're a businessperson. Why? Because a book changes your life. No matter what you do in your business, whether it is taxidermy for turkeys or helping people market themselves on the Internet (both legitimate businesses with books attached to them), you want to be perceived as the expert, and there's no quicker way of getting that "expert" tag than with a book.

So in other words, your book is your very own pair of ruby slippers. When you get to the door at Oz, and you don't have a book, then the little guy says, "Why, you're not allowed in. What business would the wizard have with you?" But when you knock on the door and he pulls back the little peephole and sees you have a book, he says, "Why, that's a horse of different color. Come on in." And in that instant you have gained access to the wonderful world of Emerald City, the land of published authors where everyone is rich, skinny, and has great hair—well, at least they have a better life.

With your book—your very own customized ruby slippers—you get to play with all the different colored horses. This is everybody in the publishing world: editors, agents, publishers, and people who are going on radio and television and could talk about your book. With a book, you're in. You're now a VIP, and you have all the privileges of a VIP: the networking opportunities, the joint venture and affiliate prospects. You also have access to a variety of smaller wizards: the TV producers, the radio guys, the editors in the top publishing houses. And sometimes you even get to see the Grand Wizard herself, Oprah!

I know all of this because I am a published author. I've made it into the inner sanctuary of the Grand Wizard, and I've promoted authors for thirty years. I've done all the things that I talk about—hundreds of radio shows, dozens of TV shows, write-ups in the *New York Times,* and a front page appearance on the *Wall Street Journal.* The company I founded more than thirty years ago, Planned TV Arts, helps writers of all shapes and colors publicize their books. I've seen it a thousand times; publishing can change your life. And as an Entrepreneurial Author, it is one of the essential items on your "to do" list that needs to be checked off sooner than later—because as an Entrepreneurial Author making your way through the minefield of marketing, you want something that makes you stand out from the rest of the folks out there who do what you do or make what you make.

PUBLISHING AS A STRATEGY

Entrepreneurial Authors are aggressive in their marketing because they find as many opportunities as they can to get their message out loud and clear to the world. What better medium to do this with than a book? A book presents many different marketing opportunities because of one significant difference. You get on radio shows and even TV shows—arenas that you don't have to pay for, by the way—because you're not talking about you; you're talking about your book.

Books give you credibility. Think about it. When you see celebrities on a talk show, they're there because they're promoting their latest movie. Authors do the same thing. It's always a much tougher sell to promote yourself. Your book is you once removed, and so it makes you more user-friendly.

Also, being an Entrepreneurial Author is about using your imagination to develop marketing strategies that will capture your target market. With the advent of Amazon, you don't even need to be in the major bookstore chains to get your book out there. I know hundreds of authors who made it to the top of Amazon and their book never once graced the aisles of Barnes and Noble. And if you are marketing your book well, you can reach your niche public much more efficiently with a book than through any other medium.

And of course, the hallmark of any Entrepreneurial Author is to use your imagination; for books, especially small, "how-to" type books, are the best kind of business card you can pass out. You give them out to people just like you do a business card, and it gives your new contact a much better picture of who you are. This helps you to build a relationship with them—another hallmark Entrepreneurial Author principle—even before you sit down with them face-to-face, because they have read all about you.

WHERE YOUR BOOK COMES FROM

Now, don't start thinking, *I'm not a writer, how could I ever publish a book?* This is the great part. You don't have to be a writer. If you reread what I've said up to this point, I've been saying published author, not published writer. You hire someone to write your book for you. Ghostwriters and editors—good ones—are worth their weight in gold because they take your story and they make it sound good. I'm not actually even the writer of this piece, but I am the author. These are my ideas that are being presented.

To put a book together, all you need to do is gather up your content in some way. Have a friend interview you. If you know anything about Internet marketing, you record a teleseminar, or a series of them; have someone transcribe what you said; and then you either edit it into book form or pay a good editor to do it. Just know you are the expert at what you do. Tell someone about it, and then put what you said into a book. Yes, it will take time, not a small amount of energy, and definitely a lot of push to get it done. That's the nature of putting a book together, and it's part of being an Entrepreneurial Author.

THE ENTREPRENEURIAL PUBLISHER

David Hancock founded Morgan James as a way to help authors leverage the power of their books to promote themselves and their businesses. It was created by an Entrepreneurial Author for Entrepreneurial Authors. From a publishing standpoint, he took the best of the traditional publishing world and combined it with all the best of the self-publishing world and made it into the best way to publish your book, with The Entrepreneurial Publisher.

Getting a book published can be daunting. It requires work to get the book done and on the shelves of bookstores everywhere.

But it's as necessary for your business as breathing, because no other marketing technique can catapult you to the big time more than having a book. So get to work. You too can have your very own pair of ruby slippers. See you in Oz!

{Introduction}

Why You Have to Be an Entrepreneurial Author

The United States is in the midst of an entrepreneurial explosion, one of the most hopeful signs for the country's future. As an author, you are an entrepreneur. Every book you write is a separate enterprise with its own fate and its own reckoning that balances income against expenditures. For Entrepreneurial Authors, the only business criteria that count are profits and relationships.

Today there are more authors than ever, but few are true Entrepreneurial Authors. If you are contemplating the life of an author, the way of The Entrepreneurial Author is the path you should follow. If you are already an author, that is the direction in which you should evolve.

Entrepreneurial Authorship did not exist for your parents or for your grandparents, because the path has only recently been blazed. Technology and enlightenment have marked its way. The

Puritan work ethic of your ancestors has gone by the wayside, along with the Puritans. That work ethic had no place for balance, only for hard work. The Entrepreneurial Author's work ethic includes both.

{ CHAPTER 1 }

The Goals

Welcome to the dawn of a new revolution. And congratulations on even considering becoming an Entrepreneurial Author in a new, rapidly changing world. It's challenging, but you're in for a lot of fun. Of course, there is a lot of work—but fun, too. Lots of fun if you do it right.

The first thing you'll notice about being an Entrepreneurial Author is that your goals will be different from the old-fashioned goals of a traditional author. The Entrepreneurial Author is flexible, innovative, unconventional, dependent, interactive, generous, enjoyable, profitable, and has low overhead costs. The goal is to stay that way.

Look at the authors all around you. If you can't see many, it's because they are not Entrepreneurial Authors; instead they're buried in work, rarely coming up for fresh air or free time. The goals of The Entrepreneurial Author allow them the freedom to pursue interests beyond work—while amassing an income beyond that of their workaholic ancestors.

You can always tell Entrepreneurial Authors by their goals. They are not as money-minded as the authors who came before them. They seem to be happier with the work that they're doing and appear to really care about satisfying the needs of their readers. You've never seen follow-up done the way these people do it. They stay in touch *constantly* with their readers. It's not as if they are working at their business, but rather demonstrating *passion* for their work. Their goal is to express that passion with excellence and transform it into profits.

Not surprisingly, Entrepreneurial Authors achieve their goals on a daily basis. Their long-term goals are lofty. Those goals exist in the future. Their short-term goals are even loftier. Those exist in the *present*—because that is the domain of the entrepreneur. That is where their goals are to be found in abundance.

Your ability to plan for the future and learn from the past will determine your level of comfort in the present, in the here and now. Being an Entrepreneurial Author means realizing that these can be the good old days and that you don't have to wait for the joy that comes with success. It's right here in front of you.

The New American Dream

Originally the dream meant having enough food and protection from the weather. Cave-dwellers dreamt of hunting enough game or gathering an abundance of nuts and berries. That dream changed, replaced by the hope of earning enough money to feed a hungry family. The Industrial Revolution took care of that and eventually gave birth to the American Dream: a house, a job, and financial security.

The Oldest American Dream

Authors of the twentieth century were motivated by a slightly different version of the American Dream. In place of a house, a job, and financial security, they sought fortune, security, expansion, and power. But that journey was characterized by a workaholic mindset, sacrifice, and greed.

The author of the twenty-first century will be more of a guerrilla—one who thrives on the nontraditional, does the unconventional if the conventional is nonsensical, and knows that working in the new millennium requires rethinking the nature of being a successful Entrepreneurial Author.

The Entrepreneurial Author will be motivated by *the journey itself,* because the journey will be the goal.

Balance will be the new dream. The Entrepreneurial Author who goes about creating a profit-producing enterprise will begin with balance, actually *starting* with work that makes them happy— the goal of all entrepreneurial dreams. Once that has been attained, The Entrepreneurial Author will be able to pursue their other goals: making money, enjoying free time, maintaining their health, and having fun.

When the journey is the goal, you can begin with work that satisfies you. You will have time to spend enjoying activities other than the work you love and a remarkable freedom from work-related stress. The Entrepreneurial Authors, many of whom exist today well ahead of their time, have twenty characteristics in common. These twenty hallmarks fuel the commitment these authors have— to themselves, their families, their communities, and their work. Here are their goals:

The Journey Is the Goal

1. *The Entrepreneurial Author knows that the journey is the goal.* He also realizes that he is in control of his enterprise, not the other way around; and if he is dissatisfied with his journey, he is missing the point of the journey itself. Unlike old-fashioned enterprises, which often required gigantic sacrifices for the sake of the goal, The Entrepreneurial Author places the goal of a pleasant journey ahead of the mere notion of sacrifices.

2. *The Entrepreneurial Author achieves balance from the very start.* She builds free time into her work schedule so that balance is part of her enterprise. She respects her leisure time as much as her work time, never allowing too much of one to interfere with the other. Traditional authors always placed work ahead of leisure

and showed no respect for their own personal freedom. Entrepreneurial Authors cherish their freedom as much as their work.

3. *The Entrepreneurial Author is not in a hurry.* Unnecessary speed frequently undermines even the best-conceived strategies. Haste makes waste and sacrifices quality. The Entrepreneurial Author is fully aware that patience is his ally, and he has planned intelligently to eliminate most emergencies that call for moving fast. His pace is always steady, but never rushed.

A Warning Sign

4. *The Entrepreneurial Author uses stress as a benchmark.* If she feels any stress, she knows she must be going about things in the wrong way. Entrepreneurial Authors do not accept stress as a part of doing business and recognize any stress as a warning sign that something's the matter—in the work plan of the author or in the business itself. Adjustments are made to eliminate the cause of the stress, which causes the stress to disappear.

5. *The Entrepreneurial Author looks forward to work.* He has a love affair with his work and considers himself blessed to be paid for doing the work that he does. He is good at his work, energizing his passion for it in a quest to learn

more about it and improve his understanding of it, thereby increasing his skills. The Entrepreneurial Author doesn't think about his retirement, because he would never want to stop doing the work he loves.

6. *The Entrepreneurial Author has no weaknesses.* She is effective in every aspect of her enterprise, because she has filled in the gaps between her strengths and talents with people who abound at the prowess she lacks. She is very much a team player and allies herself with other Entrepreneurial Authors who share the team spirit and posses complementary skills. She values her teammates as much as old-fashioned authors valued their independence.

7. *The Entrepreneurial Author is fusion-oriented.* He is always on the alert to fuse his business with other synergistic authors. He is willing to combine marketing efforts, production skills, information, leads, mailing lists, and anything else to increase his effectiveness and marketing reach while reducing the cost of achieving those goals. His fusion efforts are intentionally short-term and rarely permanent. In his business relationships, instead of thinking "marriage," he thinks "fling."

No Kidding

8. *The Entrepreneurial Author does not kid herself.* She knows that if she overestimates her own abilities, she runs the risk

of skimping on the quality she represents to her customers, employees, investors, suppliers, and fusion partners. She forces herself to face reality on a daily basis and realizes that all of her business practices must always be evaluated in the glaring light of what really is happening instead of what should be happening.

9. *The Entrepreneurial Author lives in the present.* He is well aware of the past and very enticed by the future, but the here and now is where he resides, embracing the technologies of the present, leaving future technologies on the horizon right where they belong until later when they are ripe and ready. He is alert to the new, wary of the avant-garde, and wooed from the old only by improvement, not mere change.

10. *The Entrepreneurial Author understands the precious nature of time.* She doesn't buy into that old lie that "time is money" and knows in her heart that time is far more important than money. She knows that time is life. She is aware that her customers and prospects feel the same way about time, so she respects theirs and wouldn't dare waste it. As a practicing Entrepreneurial Author, she is the epitome of efficiency, but never lets it interfere with her effectiveness.

11. *The Entrepreneurial Author always operates according to a plan.* He knows who he is, where he is going, and how he will get there. He knows why he is here in the first place.

He is prepared, knows that anything can and will happen, and can deal with the barriers to entrepreneurial success, because his plan has foreseen them and shown exactly how to surmount them. The Entrepreneurial Author reevaluates his plan regularly and does not hesitate to make changes in it, though commitment to the plan is part of his very being.

A Guide, Not a Master

12. *The Entrepreneurial Author is flexible.* She is guided by a strategy for success and knows the difference between a guide and a master. When it is necessary, The Entrepreneurial Author changes, accepting change is part of the status quo, not ignoring or battling it. She is able to adapt to new situations, realizes that service is whatever her customers want it to be, and knows that inflexible things become brittle and break.

13. *The Entrepreneurial Author aims for results more than growth.* He is focused on profitability and balance, vitality and improvement, and value and quality more than size and growth. His plan calls for steadily increasing profits without the sacrifice of personal time, so his actions are oriented to hitting those targets instead of growing for the sake of growth alone. He is

wary of becoming large and does not equate hugeness with excellence.

A Little Help from Friends

14. *The Entrepreneurial Author is dependent upon many people.* She knows that the age of the lone-wolf author—independent and proud of it—has passed. The Entrepreneurial Author is very dependent upon her fusion business partners, her employees, her customers, her suppliers, and her mentors. She got where she is with her own wings, her own determination, and her own smarts, as an Entrepreneurial Author with a little help from a lot of friends.

15. *The Entrepreneurial Author is constantly learning.* A seagull flies in circles in the sky, looking for food in an endless quest. When it finally finds the food, the seagull lands and eats its fill. When it has completed the meal it then returns to the sky, only to fly in circles again, searching for food, although it has eaten. Humans have only one comparable instinct—the need for constant learning. Entrepreneurial Authors have this need in spades.

16. *The Entrepreneurial Author is passionate about work.* Her enthusiasm for what she does is apparent to everyone who sees her work. This enthusiasm spreads to everyone who works with her, even to her customers. In its purest form,

this enthusiasm is best expressed as the word *passion*—an intense feeling that burns within her and is manifested in the devotion she demonstrates toward her business.

17. *The Entrepreneurial Author is focused on the goal.* He knows that balance does not come easily and that he must rid himself of the values and expectations of his ancestors. To do this, he must remain focused on his journey, seeing the future clearly while concentrating on the present. He is aware that the minutia of life and business can distract him, so he does what is necessary to make those distractions only momentary.

18. *The Entrepreneurial Author is disciplined about the tasks at hand.* She is keenly aware that every time she writes a task on her daily calendar, she is making a promise to herself. As an Entrepreneurial Author who does not kid herself, she keeps those promises, knowing that the achievement of her goals will be more than an adequate reward for her discipline. She finds it easy to be disciplined because of the payback offered by the leisure that follows.

19. *The Entrepreneurial Author is well-organized at home and at work.* He does not waste valuable time looking for items that have been misplaced and stays organized as he works and as new work comes to him. His astute sense of order is fueled by the efficiency that results from it. He shares his

ability to organize with those who work with him. Yet The Entrepreneurial Author never squanders precious time by becoming overly organized.

20. *The Entrepreneurial Author has an upbeat attitude.* Because she knows that life is unfair, that problems arise, that to error is human, and that the cool shall inherit the Earth, she manages to take obstacles in stride, keeping her perspective and her sense of humor. Her ever-present optimism is grounded in an ability to perceive the positive side of things—recognizing the negative but never dwelling on it, her positive attitude is contagious and spreads rapidly.

Life as a Fairy Tale

Perhaps in the light of these twenty criteria, you're thinking, "Do Entrepreneurial Authors exist in real life or only in fairy tales?" The answer is yes. They do exist in real life, but their success and balance are like a fairy tale. They exist all around you.

Armed with the right vision and the right information, The Entrepreneurial Author can attain heights never before envisioned. They can add the element of love to their work, because they will devote themselves only to work that they love.

This book has been written to make the dream vividly clear to you. If you can see the dream, you can will it to come true. If you can will it to come true, you can take the steps to empower your will with actions.

The Entrepreneurial Author does more than read books and attend seminars about achievement and success. They take action, do something, and shake the tree. They know that their time on Earth is limited, that the most important time is *right now,* and that they've got to get it right the first time. To do this, they go with the flow— *their own flow*— possessing the sensitivity to know what they really want, what they can do well, why they're here, what they love to do, what is realistic, and what is possible.

The Art of the Possible

The Entrepreneurial Author is a master of the *art of the possible.*

What is written in these pages is all possible. We didn't have the benefit of a book to plant these ideas in our heads, but we made them up as we went along or realized them as we looked back.

It won't take you long to recognize that you have all the makings of an Entrepreneurial Author, that you can do what we are writing about, that you can live your dream, that you can work with joy, and that it won't take you a bundle to get you started—or even a lot of time.

The Goals of The Entrepreneurial Author

The goals of The Entrepreneurial Author are loftier than those of the traditional author: attaining work that is satisfying, enough money to enjoy freedom from worry about it, health good enough to take for granted, a family or bonding with others with whom you can give and receive love and support, fun that does not have to be pursued but exists in daily living, and the longevity to appreciate with wisdom that you and those you love have achieved.

Most importantly, as I hope you realize, the goal of The Entrepreneurial Author is the journey itself.

Entrepreneurial Authors set their sights on attaining these goals as they live their dream of enjoying life and the attainment of them. This has not been the way with most traditional authors.

Simply observing the economy, unemployment statistics, the plight of the homeless, and the low level of job satisfaction among the employed—along with their secret nightmare of becoming laid off during a massive downsizing—vividly proves that our society isn't living up to its potential as a successful civilization.

Ten U-turns

At least ten reasons explain this situation. We've been led down ten garden paths that lead to the economic and social swamp in which we find ourselves mired at the moment. The time has come for us to make ten U-turns. Forget what the signs say and what your parents and teachers said about those supposedly one-way streets. U-turns are highly recommended for any traveler who wants to reach the destination, not to mention thoroughly enjoy the journey.

TEN DIRTY LIES
YOU HAVE KNOWN AND LOVED

1. *Time is money.* This is a blatant untruth, made up by those who are on hourly wages—frequently minimum wage. Time is far more valuable than money. If you run out of money, there are many ways to get more. If you run out of time, you can't get more.

The Result of Poor Planning

2. *Owning a business means being a workaholic.* People who are workaholics prefer work to every other activity, including spending time with friends and family and interests beyond work. Being a workaholic is the direct result of poor planning. Owning a business should not mean that a business owns you.

3. *Marketing is expensive.* Actually, bad marketing is expensive, and good marketing is inexpensive. Entrepreneurial

Authors wouldn't think of using expensive marketing, but they know they must get the word out about their businesses. So they utilize inexpensive marketing with skill and fervor, using time, energy, and imagination instead of the brute force of megabucks.

Wombs and Tombs

4. *Big corporations are like wombs.* Big corporations used to be like wombs, but these days many are like tombs. They employ the living dead, who work with devotion yet will be squeezed out, kicking and screaming, because of merging, downsizing, cost-cutting, restructuring, and bankruptcy. If you want a corporation that functions like a womb, form it yourself.

5. *Youth is better than age.* People who believe this one are usually young. Getting old means trading in some abilities to acquire others. It means losing some body power but gaining mind power, and not making the same mistake twice—or even once. It also helps you understand yourself and realize what wisdom really is.

6. *You need a job.* You need work, no doubt about it. And a job, structured by someone other than yourself, is one form of work. But the truth for most people is that you do *not* need a standard nine-to-five job working for someone

other than yourself—and if you do, expect to pay a high price: abdicating your freedom and the discovery of your unique essence. But you do need work, and work should help you enjoy your freedom and discover your essential talents. Entrepreneurial Authors love their work, but they're usually jobless. They establish the structure of their work rather than relying on an employer.

7. *Heaven is only in the afterlife.* Heaven can be here and now if you know where to look for it. Living your life as though heaven existed only somewhere else and in some other time means missing the point of your life. Instead, live this life so that the heaven that follows has a lot to live up to.

Learning to Love Learning

8. *The purpose of education is to teach facts.* The real purpose of education is to teach people to love learning. The more you love learning, the better informed you'll be throughout your life. Constant learning will always be your ally. The Entrepreneurial Author realizes that times are always changing and that growing up is a process that never should end.

9. *Retirement is a good thing.* Pay close attention here: retirement can be fatal. It often leads to inactivity, which

can lead to an early demise. If you desire longevity, don't consider total retirement. People who completely retire shut down vital systems in their hearts, minds, souls, and spirits. It's okay to cut down on your workload—even to cut down drastically. But never eliminate it. Don't forget that the way of The Entrepreneurial Author is characterized by balance, and retirement can lead to imbalance—not to mention boredom.

10. *If you want it done right, do it yourself.* This is the battle cry of the terminal workaholic. The battle cry of The Entrepreneurial Author is, "Don't do anything you can properly delegate." It is usually unwise to think nobody can do things right except you. Such a mindset means you lack the ability to train or to link with others—mandatory skills of The Entrepreneurial Author.

Once you're free of the shackles of these ten lies, you can focus on your goals—one key to succeeding as an Entrepreneurial Author. To reach your goals, you must not only be aware of them, but also acknowledge that goals change.

An Ugly Ally

While striving for your goals, you will form a friendship with an ugly ally, one you will try to avoid. But as an Entrepreneurial Author who takes risks, you will not be unable to avoid it forever.

This ally is called *failure*. Get to know it, because if you take pains to eliminate it entirely, you will live a boring life indeed.

Failure is part of the deal when you're an Entrepreneurial Author. Just because failure is instructive and has a lesson tucked neatly into it doesn't mean it's any fun. But Entrepreneurial Authors learn to construct safety nets in the form of alternative sources of income, so failure isn't the ogre it used to be.

The Entrepreneurial Author generates several streams of income to support their life. If one stream dries up, financial nourishment comes from another stream. No single stream may produce enough income, but together they create a mighty river. This enables The Entrepreneurial Author to tap several of their abilities.

Is it Okay to Break the Rules?

Does it seem as though I am asking you to break the rules in order to become a flourishing Entrepreneurial Author? Well, yes. You've got it right. The United States was shaped by rule-breakers— Ben Franklin, Tom Paine, Thomas Jefferson, Abraham Lincoln, Andrew Carnegie, Henry Ford, John D. Rockefeller, J.P. Morgan … and you? I sure hope so.

Living for the Long Term

Bill Gates, the co-founder of Microsoft, is a pretty successful rule-breaker himself. On the topic of starting one's own company, he says, "The things you know and love and see opportunities in—you ought to pick your business based on that." Sure, you can make a pile of money doing something for the short term, but the problem is the long term. You're not living life for the short term. If you were, you'd get burned out and stressed out doing work that you *have* to do rather than work that you *love* to do.

Measuring Success as an Entrepreneurial Author

Success at work for The Entrepreneurial Author will be a lot more fulfilling than success at work for the traditional author. Authors not happy with their work will be doing something wrong. If they're earning more money than they've ever imagined but are not content, they most assuredly are not The Entrepreneurial Author successes. Success for The Entrepreneurial Author will be measured by inner satisfaction more than any other criterion.

Inner satisfaction is something you get not by seeking it, but by seeking work that ignites your passion—and then doing that work. It is a realization that occurs rather than a consciously sought attainment. But you won't realize it by chasing money or even by getting money, no matter how much you make.

Along with inner satisfaction, The Entrepreneurial Author will orient his business toward being with his family—the small nuclear family of the twentieth century, as well as the larger extended family of the twenty-first century. He will become part of his community, whether that community is his neighborhood, his industry, or his ever-expanding online world. He will obtain much of the fun he needs from the work he does, but will recognize that he needs recreation beyond work. Surely the old goals of financial independence, control of his destiny, and recognition of his talents will motivate him. But he will also be drawn to a newer goal best described as *innovation* or *discovery.* He will want to contribute to society with more than his time or money. He will find ways to do this through the work he does, because Entrepreneurial Authors are resourceful. In fact, resourcefulness is a survival technique of The Entrepreneurial Author.

The Entrepreneurial Author's Roadmap

The Entrepreneurial Author is able to succeed on the journey by having a clear and simple roadmap. Signposts illuminate the road. Here's what they say:

* Learn
* Cooperate
* Focus
* Feel Passion
* Delegate
* Share
* Respect Time
* Bend

* Profit
* See

These signposts enable Entrepreneurial Authors to select their pace and never lose their way. Entrepreneurial Authors realize that even after they have passed a sign, they continue to move in the right direction. They keep in mind the words on these additional signposts:

* Plan
* Manage
* Market
* Sell
* Serve
* Satisfy
* Relate
* Globalize
* Improve
* Be Cool

What Promotes Happiness

Since Entrepreneurial Authors strive to achieve inner satisfaction, the components of happiness are well known to them. In his book, *The Pursuit of Happiness,* author David Myers, sounding a lot like an Entrepreneurial Author, cites ten items that promote happiness:

1. A fit and healthy body
2. Realistic goals and expectations

3. Positive self-esteem

4. Feelings of control

5. Optimism

6. Outgoingness

7. Supportive friendships

8. An intimate, sexually warm marriage of equals

9. Challenging work and active leisure coupled with adequate rest and retreat

10. Spiritual faith

We are living in a time when people are seeking to pursue less demanding careers. People are taking a new look at the meaning of success. They no longer automatically assume that the only way to be successful is to always be moving up the corporate ladder or to be burning the midnight oil.

A whole new set of rules is emerging. To succeed in the past, all you had to do was follow orders and perform the same routine tasks day after day. In the future and in the present, what you have to do is identify and solve problems quickly.

The First Rule of the Future

Here is the first rule of the future: Be *prepared* to change *collars.* The man in the gray flannel suit with a white-collar job no longer has the job due to the surgical elimination of layers of management. As I write this, 9,600 people per day are being laid off in the United States. That same man, now without a job, doesn't wear a gray flannel suit anymore because the era of the technician is upon us, and technicians don't wear suits. He no longer wears a white collar, because it is increasingly being recognized as garb of the past. And most importantly, he is probably not a man in the first place since so many women are swelling the ranks of entrepreneurial America.

A Spawning Ground
for Entrepreneurial Authors

Here is the second rule of the future: *Learn to love your network.* In the past, Americans would measure success by their ability to climb the corporate ladder. But the ladder exists no more. Success is measured by the results of your creativity, your autonomy, and your ability to devise a new solution, develop a new idea, or deliver a new service. Often success is achieved by teams. At the conclusion of a project, the teams disband and the people move to other teams. The ladder is now a network—an infinite number of paths that ultimately connect with many others. Rather than trudge from one rung to the next on a rigid upward course, you can connect with others at lightning speed and then disconnect when your purposes have been achieved. The larger your network, the more work will come your way. The better you treat other members in your network, the better they'll treat you. As in the past, people who are fun to work with will be a premium. Prima donnas and mean-spirited high achievers need not apply in the world of The Entrepreneurial Author.

It's a Wired World

Here is the third rule of the future: *It's a wired world; deal with it.* The Internet is growing at a faster rate than TV grew during its fastest growth spurt. The Internet is a place for fun and profit, work and play, data and wisdom, love and friendship, networking and going it alone—it's a hotbed for Entrepreneurial Authors. It allows people to go to almost anyplace on the planet. A lot of working in the future will consist of collaborations strictly by computer network.

A Skill-Eat-Skill Economy

Here's the fourth rule of the future: *What you earn depends more than ever upon what you learn.* You can do your learning at a college or technical school, in training on the job, or by investing in seminars and books. Security no longer comes from sticking with one company for an entire career, but by maintaining a portfolio of flexible skills. That's why there are so many universities out there offering lifelong learning classes for students from college age through golden age, online and offline. The new economy will not be a dog-eat-dog economy, but a skill-eat-skill economy. The more skills you have and the better trained you are with the skills you have, the more success you will achieve—pure cause and effect.

In Search of Excellence author Tom Peters calls Entrepreneurial Authors to action. He says, "Build your own firm, and create your own network—it's that or bust."

Care Like Crazy

Says Peters of the future, "Add it up and you get something rather surprising. There's no rejection of the past in all this! Expertise is more important than ever, not less. And bigness has its place. However, expertise is being changed, altered almost beyond recognition. If you're not skilled/motivated/passionate about something, you're in trouble!" Notice this: the man did not say what you're to be skilled, or motivated, or passionate about— that's for you to determine. He only advises that you *care like crazy* about it.

Deepak Chopra, author of *Ageless Body, Timeless Mind,* also speaks of what you should care like crazy about. He suggests simply that you ask yourself, "If I had all the time and money in the world, what would I do?" If you persist in asking that question, the answer will come to you; and when it tells you what it is, then do *that thing.* He says that if you do, you will have all the money and time that you will ever need.

Chopra, who also wrote *The Seven Spiritual Laws of Success,* offers this advice to would-be Entrepreneurial Authors, and I wish I could print it in neon ink for you, or at least make it last within the annals of your retinal system forever: "There is one thing each of us has that no one else has. There is one thing you can do that nobody else can. Find it, and foster it. You will never die at your business if you are doing what you are meant to do."

Merely doing it is the start to achieving success as an Entrepreneurial Author.

Integrating Your Business with Your Life

One of the *most* pleasurable—yet difficult—tasks for an Entrepreneurial Author to achieve and maintain is living in the moment. You've got to begin that task right now, as you read this book, if you're to become an Entrepreneurial Author! To do so, you'll have to let go of your old notions of work and leisure. It will mean dismantling those compartments into which you—or more likely, your great-grandparents—have divided your life.

In doing this, you'll free yourself to do things that matter to you. If you're a spiritual person and you get in touch with God at church, synagogue, temple, or while reading the Bible, you'll be able to be your spiritual self whenever and wherever you want. If you want to spend more time with your family, you'll be able to. One of the greatest rewards of being an Entrepreneurial Author will be the chance for people to recognize the pure nobility of work when it is pursued with joy rather than obligation. But work of the future will not be an obsession as it is right now. It will be part of a well-balanced existence. You will have many better things to do than work. Oscar Wilde once said, "Work is the refuge of people who have nothing better to do."

Step Back a Few Paces

Now, Entrepreneurial Authors are stepping back a few paces and seeing that work is not the entire picture. Other parts of that picture include: recreation, friends, family, faith, health, location, education, travel, and free time. Have I left anything out? Probably. It's a big and beautiful picture. These are the rewards of living. The rewards should not be reserved for your retirement, because Entrepreneurial Authors never completely retire from work. They may cut back, but they're having too much of a blast to retire. As Entrepreneurial Authors, they want to use their longevity for meeting and savoring the elixir of surmounting new challenges as time, technology, and they themselves undergo staggering changes. As much as they feel passion for their work, Entrepreneurial Authors never allow it to erode the other joys of living. The elixir recipe calls for enjoying life while earning a living.

Ten Entrepreneurial Author Attitudes

In order to integrate your business with your life, exactly what do you need? You must have ten attitudes and ten pieces of real equipment. These are the ten attitudes:

1. Organization
2. Determination
3. Discipline
4. Passion
5. Love of Life
6. Optimism
7. Flexibility
8. Honesty
9. Self-esteem
10. Generosity

What is the cost of these ten attitudes? The only cost is giving up old ideas, old habits, and old weaknesses. The cost of the ten pieces of real equipment is about $2,500—probably less if you shop online, and you don't need all the equipment at first. These are the ten items:

1. Computer
2. Printer
3. High-speed Internet access
4. Word processing software
5. Fax machine
6. Telephone
7. Voice mail
8. Cell phone
9. Scanner
10. Phone lines for your phone and fax machine

Simplicity of Work Style

Entrepreneurial Author businesses thrive as virtual companies. They embrace the technology that allows them this freedom, and then they prosper in their businesses and the other important aspects of their lives. It wasn't always as easy to run a virtual company. If it were, you'd have learned about being an Entrepreneurial Author from your grandparents. They also would have loved the benefits of integrating their business with their lives. But they didn't have the choice that you do.

Maintaining Balance

Although I wish to make the life of an Entrepreneurial Author sound interesting, challenging, and rewarding to you, I wish to lead you not into temptation, but to deliver you from evil.

The temptation will be success. When it comes, you're going to be nuts about it, and you'll want more of it—the deluxe version. Go for it. But don't go with so much gusto that you destroy the balance of life.

The evil will be in your reactions to success. You may become an effective author. You might change focus from the path of The Entrepreneurial Author to the path of the work slave. Or worst of all, you might continue working without a plan.

Balance is the key to keeping temptations and evils at bay. It is the critical difference between an Entrepreneurial Author and a traditional author. An Entrepreneurial Author knows that unless balance is part of the overall plan—right from the start—it's only going to be a word and never a style of living. Balance is very difficult to achieve if it's something you figure you'll get down the road. If you were on a high wire, balance is not something you'd settle for *eventually.* You'd want it always. You'd want it now. Life in these times is a high wire.

Five Kinds of Work

Entrepreneurial Authors not only balance their work time with leisure time, learning time, family time, and time for anything else they want to do, they also balance their work time itself. And they've learned that there are five kinds of work:

1. *Wage work* is job work in the scenario. You sell your time to those employing you, and they manage your time. At one time, this work made the most sense for people. Your grandparents lived during that time, but it has passed. Wage work is nonsense for over half the people doing it now.

2. *Fee work* is professional work. Professionals in many fields charge a fee for the work they do and for their time—which is then spent the way they want, when they want, under their own management. People who work as consultants for businesses charge fees; they don't earn wages. This makes the businesses *and* the professional individuals satisfied.

3. *Housework* is the work done on and for the home. It's work that has to be done, such as cooking, cleaning, and shopping, and is ordinarily unpaid. These days, it is rapidly being redistributed from women to men. At the same time, it is more appreciated and is important enough to be part of the well-balanced work portfolio.

4. *Study work* is educational work. Self-improvement by way of an advanced degree or extra certification is more important than ever as more people discover that an additional degree or certificate gives them an edge in the working world. Entrepreneurial Authors study to improve in many areas aside from work. Human understanding is part of what they learn.

5. *Volunteer work* is free work. You do this work for causes such as schools, hospitals, religious groups, political groups, charities, and sport groups. The income you derive from this work is emotional, spiritual, and permanent. To many people, it is more gratifying than financial income.

Entrepreneurial Authors try to engage in all five kinds of work, knowing the benefits of each one will help them maintain balance. Wage work offers security, fee work provides the joy of being paid for your talent and knowledge, housework keeps you grounded, study work is an investment in yourself, and volunteer work is the taxes paid by your body to your soul.

A Built-in Balance Provider

How could you possibly fit all five kinds of work into your life? It's easy when you *plan at the outset.* Planning is a built-in balance provider. It helps ensure that you'll have time to help at home, to learn about life, and to help others while you bring home the bacon with your other pursuits—a regular gig a few days a week or even once a month. If you do too much of any one kind of work, you'll be out of balance, and the work will almost instantly cease to be much fun. Entrepreneurial Authors achieve balance as a matter of choice, not as a matter of necessity.

Who leads the way in living unbalanced lives? Workaholics top the list. They often believe that unless they do their work immediately, the universe will come to a grinding halt. High achievers who sacrifice freedom come next on the list of the unbalanced; they intentionally abandon balance for the sake of fame or fortune. Fame and fortune do have their price, but balance need not be part of it. Kids grow up only once. If you miss it the first time, there's no rerun.

Some experts believe that workaholics are dying faster than alcoholics. This may not be readily apparent because so many workaholics watch their nutrition and exercise. They look great and may even work out regularly, but that only prolongs their ability to remain workaholics. They aren't listening to their bodies telling them something is wrong, so it takes something like a massive coronary to get their attention.

World-Class Listeners

Entrepreneurial Authors are exceptional listeners. They listen to their readers, to their mentors, to their friends, and to their kids. They listen to their parents and certainly to their teachers. They also listen to their bodies, their inner voice, and the voice of reason. They never allow the past to dictate the future. In the past world of work, balance had no part, just as the idea of having enough time was not appreciated until the late 1980s. Although the idea of balance is finally on the forefront of the American mind, it is still a clouded notion, still a new concept, and still considered an unattainable dream to many people. We believe that only two factors are required to achieve balance: to *imagine it,* and then to *commit* to it. Imagining it can be harder than committing to it. Once visualized, it is a relative cinch to commit to it.

Entrepreneurial Author Intelligence

You'll find it relatively easy to maintain balance if you begin with it. Start out with it—*no matter what.* Don't delude yourself into thinking that you can switch gears later. Many have tried. Most have failed. Entrepreneurial Authors are so enamored with the idea of balance that they wouldn't dream of losing sight of their target before they let the arrows fly. They know that once the arrows are in full flight, you can't say to them, "Okay, hang a left turn now!"

As an Entrepreneurial Author, you're shooting an arrow. You get to take aim in any direction you want. If that direction does not include balance, you'll misfire. You will not be following the way of The Entrepreneurial Author.

You realize by now that being an Entrepreneurial Author is far more than pure work. It's really a work style, a lifestyle, a living style, a behavior style, a values style, and a priorities style.

Loving Your Leisure

If you don't have leisure activities that you love as much as your work, if you don't have a family or relationships that you enjoy every bit as much as your work, if you don't have the time to engage in leisure or bask in relationships, you're no Entrepreneurial Author. Those are the elements that provide balance. You need them for equilibrium as much as you need the work itself.

The Yardstick for Measuring the Success of a Business

The first factor in measuring the success of your business is to assess your inner satisfaction to determine whether you are enjoying the process of being in business or even enjoying being alive. The second factor is to ascertain that your business meshes well with your life as it does with your essence—who you really are. The third factor is to determine whether or not you have balance in your life.

And there's a fourth measurement of your success—*after* you've arranged to have enough free time, *after* you've found ways to contribute to your planet, *after* you've formed your connections, *after* your relationships are in order, and *after* your health is excellent. This measuring method should be part of your overall plan or you'll lose your way.

The yardstick to which I refer is *profit,* the lifeblood of an author. Entrepreneurial Authors keep their eyes on that bottom line, but they never lose their awareness of their higher priorities.

Amazingly, some authors *never* address this crucial yardstick. Even more ridiculous, many authors make this the *only* criterion of their success. The way of The Entrepreneurial Author gives this measure of success a modified priority. Entrepreneurial Authors are inevitably interested in this measurement because it is an important part of why they are in business in the first place. But they never give profits the highest priority, because profits are neither the only nor the most important reason for being in business.

More Important than Profit

Here are ten things that true Entrepreneurial Authors consider to be more important than profit:

1. Their future
2. Their overall plan
3. Their readers
4. Their employees
5. Their prospects
6. Their families
7. Their time
8. Their inner satisfaction
9. Their integration of business and life
10. Their balance

Less Important than Profit

Now here are ten things that true Entrepreneurial Authors consider less important than profit:

1. Their sales
2. Their returns
3. Their response rate
4. Their store traffic
5. Their volume
6. Their gross
7. Their press coverage
8. Their ego
9. Their status quo
10. Their growth

Entrepreneurial Authors emphasize profitability.

Entrepreneurial Authors
Don't Kid Themselves

They manage to do this because they never kid themselves. They know that bigger isn't necessarily better, that expensive isn't necessarily worth the extra expense. They perform two primary jobs that increase their profits:

* They improve everything they do.
* They eliminate any mistakes entirely.

Entrepreneurial Authors have a wide definition of *everything*—it consists of anything connected to their business, inside and out. They have an equally broad definition of *mistakes*. Anything that is not done with excellence is a mistake. Entrepreneurial Authors are not perfectionists; they know that perfectionists cause stress for others and can be ineffective in their use of time. But Entrepreneurial Authors do have high standards and noble expectations. They expect those standards to be met with exception. They take for granted that their expectations will be met and often exceeded.

The Entrepreneurial Author knows that improvement increases profits and that mistakes decrease profits.

Sharing Your Profits Generously

Earlier, we investigated profit in terms of financial gain; now, we're going to switch mental gears, open our souls, and view profit from a wider perspective.

There is a business profit other than money. The joy of accomplishment is something that most authors are deprived of, but something that transcends income. Money is one type of payment for work well done; praise and recognition provide a different kind of payment. Successes should be shared with agents, editors, publicists, others in your network, and certainly staff. Profits should be shared with your community, your industry, your city, and your nation. Rewards should be used to support the arts, education, the environment, charities that you care about, and the needy. Think in terms of sharing your largesse with the planet. This will add momentum to your profile while contributing to the betterment of humankind.

Profit-sharing will take on a vastly expanded meaning as the twenty-first century develops and as participation and community become criteria for success in business. Entrepreneurial Authors are already learning that social responsibility and environmental awareness form part of the bottom line, along with all those dollars and cents. Warmth toward fellow beings is also part of it. Many a person would happily have the recognition for a job well done more than merely the money.

The Power of Recognition

That recognition can come in many forms, not just money and words of praise, award plaques and titles, or corner offices and assistants. The profits that come in the form of repeat business, referral business, growth from within, and respect from the community or industry should be shared with anyone who even slightly contributed to them. The Entrepreneurial Author's mindset is characterized by *wanting* to share, to let others stand in the spotlight, and to spread the benefits.

This attitude is not merely the glowing realization that the more you give, the more you get. It isn't centered on payoffs to the author. The idea underlying generosity in an entrepreneurial sense is the powerful glue of *shared values.*

The Backbone of Any Business

It's not very difficult to see that the people attracted to Entrepreneurial Authorship will be those who don't mind sharing. The Entrepreneurial Author knows that the backbone of any business is its people, and that those people aren't necessarily going to be their staff. Instead, they will be a wide variety of people. Knowledge of what those people want paves the way for the author. Along with that knowledge must come a talent for listening—and caring.

Listening and caring are not tough talents to develop if you are genuinely interested in people. An interest in people will be mandatory for The Entrepreneurial Author, because the age of the lone-wolf author is well behind us. The more dependent you are, the better equipped you will be to prosper and flourish in a business of your own.

You will be dependent upon readers, to be sure, but the range of your dependency will be far broader than that of authors who have preceded you. You will probably depend, for information if not for something else, on others on the Internet. You will also depend on your family for helping you keep your working environment—possibly your home—conducive to accomplishment.

Interdependence

Interdependence is a byword of the twenty-first century because of improved communications technology and a huge growth spurt in the number of independent workers. They will relate to each other, not as employee to employer, but as human to human, each making life a little easier for the other. The giving of rewards will become commonplace, as society replaces one g-word—*greed*—with another: *generosity.* Enlightened authors in tomorrow's society will ask what they can give to others and will come up with answers such as time, money, recognition, a special parking space, a larger office, improved technology, connection to an existing network, responsibility, a club membership, or a new title—the list continues and will be enlarged.

The Entrepreneurial Author seeks these rewards—not to keep, but to give; not to own, but to grant. The mindset of giving will lead us out of the gimme-gimme-gimme past and into the better-to-give-than-receive future.

Money in this New Millennium

Money is not the root of all evil. What the Bible actually says is that the *love of money* is the root of all evil, and what George Bernard Shaw really said is *that lack of money* is the root of all evil. Money itself is completely innocent of all charges.

We have stated and reiterated that information is the currency of this new century. That is the truth. And it is your first indication that money will come in many forms as we grow. The biggest change between the twentieth century and the twenty-first century comes not in money, but in the way we perceive money and how much we allow it to dictate our lives. Although important, money will not be the top item on our mission statement if we are Entrepreneurial Authors. Enough money will be one goal, but more than enough money can get you in trouble.

The Most Emotionally Charged Business Issue

As an Entrepreneurial Author, you will find that money is the most emotionally charged business issue. You will also witness a relaxation of the emotional connection with money—the attitude that spawns greed.

Money triggers a unique behavioral response in most individuals. This response is not rooted in the more civilized parts of our brain where rationality reigns, but comes from a more primitive part where there is no room for sanity or sense. The response is actually instinctive—part of a survival mechanism.

Columbia University conducted a study of people's behavior concerning money. They set up hidden cameras in banks and then observed the video. They noticed that smiling people stopped smiling the moment they entered a bank. Animated and extroverted people stopped gesturing and became more introverted when they came within the confines of a bank. Panning around the faces, observers could see a noticeable absence of smiles and a definite presence of grimness. The study showed that people are more solemn at a bank than they are in church.

Might this study demonstrate a worship of money, a deep-seated feeling that money is holy? Or does it indicate a sense of smallness when compared with the wealth of the bank? It probably confirms all of these things.

Fortunately, although money is still necessary for survival, it is not part of our DNA; with the increasing desire for other types of success, it will become less of a motivator of human behavior.

The Entrepreneurial Author is a person in business, a person devoted to earning profits, and a person involved with matters that connect—directly or indirectly—with money. He is not emotionally connected to money, but he realizes that his prospects and his readers do not share this attitude. Most of them are still emotionally tied up with M-O-N-E-Y, and he'll have to remember that when dealing with them.

Money Is Like Manure

Entrepreneurial Authors realize that money fits into their grand scheme of generosity. They know well the words of the poet Carl Sandburg, "Money is like manure—good only when spread around." And beneath it all, at their *own* bottom line, they are aware of the truth of the words of the economist who said, "Solvency is entirely a matter of temperament and not of income." Entrepreneurial Authors have an evolved temperament in matters of money. Their yardsticks are beyond the financial ones.

{ CHAPTER 2 }

The Setting

Think of yourself as an Entrepreneurial Author, working either from a special room in your home, a room brimming with all the working technology you'll need, or from an office space, peopled with comfortably clad co-workers, far more efficient yet less formal than the office space of the past.

Perhaps the setting for your work is a high-rise building smack-dab in the middle of town. Maybe it's on an island in the middle of a lake at the edge of a large city. Possibly it's in an office area above the residential area in the building where you live, or it's on a boat heading for Fiji, of all places, and there you are, communicating using satellites, your Internet connection, and your trusty computer.

As an Entrepreneurial Author, the setting for your work will be of your own choosing. The best thing about your setting will be the things you have in it, your technological stuff to save you time and energy. The people with whom you work seem to be on your wavelength more than people of the past. Entrepreneurial Authors have a way of attracting like-minded people.

If you are still forced to travel to work, your commute will allow you to achieve your goals, whatever they may be. Although the world will be highly efficient, the stress of working in it will be noticeably lower because of the burden taken up by technology.

The life of an Entrepreneurial Author will provide you with an optimum blend of the old—valued co-workers, leisure time, opportunities to be with your family—and the new—evolved communications such as a link to the Internet and a computer that will save you loads of time. It will place you where you want to be, not where your boss says you should be. And it will enable you to awaken each morning looking forward to your workday, rather than dreading it.

If this sounds a bit as if you are living in your own dream, you are seeing clearly the way of The Entrepreneurial Author.

Business in the New Millennium

You can be sure of two things in the twenty-first century: business will be a lot harder, and business will be a lot easier.

It will be harder because of five factors:

1. *Time*

Time will become magnified in importance. The luxury of spare time at work is a luxury of the past. Spare time will be revered, but not at work. You will notice that almost everyone will share the new awareness of time. Readers will demand and expect speed. You will too.

2. *Contact*

Less face-to-face contact will remove much of the social warmth of working. People now get more than half their messages by other forms of communication, such as voicemail, e-mail, and postings to social media sites. Such communications can be misunderstood or inaccurate; verbal accuracy will grow in value. The joy of social interaction will be diminished.

3. *Change*

Change will be thrust upon us, and much that we counted on before will no longer hold forth. Even things we learn will be true only for a short time before being surpassed by new truths. Genius will not consist of learning something but in learning one thing after another. If you can't adapt, you aren't cut out to be an Entrepreneurial Author.

4. *Talent*

Talent will become diffused as top people trade the vitality of a huge corporation for the tranquility of working at home. This is well and good for them, but for Entrepreneurial Authors, this means all the big brains won't be under one roof. You'll have to scout them out.

5. *Technology*

Technology will be more important in your life, and you'll have to understand it to take full advantage of it. But technology is becoming easier to use, user manuals are written more clearly, and the nature of training (repetition will be your friend for life) has improved. If you're technophobic, see a techno-shrink.

There are really five thousand ways in which business will be easier in this new millennium, but for purposes of time and space, let's just discuss five here:

1. *Time*

You will have more time to do what really must be done, rather than wasting time with busywork, because of technological advancements. Your network of independent contractors will also free up more of your time. Use it to increase your profits, to make your business better, or to just plain enjoy yourself.

2. *Values*

Values will change, and they will be more in keeping with your own guerrilla values. In the twentieth century, the main value was making money. In the twenty-first century, this priority will take a back seat to the human values of happiness at work, free time, family, and spirituality. As you are discovering, profit-seeking will never be eliminated, only reprioritized.

3. *Advancements*

New advancements in business—physical, psychological, and technological—will make the workplace more exciting, easier to use, and even enjoyable. Flextime and teleconferencing will make for less crowded commuting, if you commute at all. The virtual office is the at-home office.

4. *Procedures*

Streamlined procedures will keep your work life efficient, organized, simple, and fast. You won't waste time or effort at work because you'll have learned to become an efficient working machine, and as an Entrepreneurial Author, you'll realize that the whole purpose of streamlining is to add *effectiveness*.

5. *People*

You will deal with smarter—but fewer—people. Your workplace won't be populated with paper-shufflers. Your at-home business will put you into contact with bright, talented entrepreneurs who made the break from the corporate life and are doing very well, just like you.

Yet even with all the changes, positive and negative, business in the new millennium will be one millennium tougher than it used to be because of greater complexity, tougher competition (and more of it), better information, more enlightened people, more educated players, new technology, and changes whizzing by faster than ever before.

Does that mean that everything is changing and everything is going to be new? It does not, though some people will fall into the fool's pit of thinking all the new rules have changed. Five fundamental things will not change, and although they may change in the far distant future, the rate of their change will be so slow that you'll be better off thinking of them as nearly static.

What Won't Change

1. Human Nature

People will be people, with the usual strengths and foibles. They will be creatures of their emotions, even though their brains will have evolved, and they will still want to be treated fairly and kindly.

2. Wants, Needs, and Fears

People will continue to want and need love and security, money and power, a sense of identity, and a feeling of well-being. They will fear the same things they fear now: lack of control, illness, and absence of love and security.

3. Youth and Age

They'll be just as they are now: young people will still be the first to try new things, and old people will still control most of the wealth. The generation gap will never close, but it will move. Every child will still grow up to be either like their parents or as a reaction to their parents.

4. *Faith*

Although people will differ in how they find faith, they will continue to seek it and continue to find it. Faith will continue to motivate the best that is within people. There will be a renaissance as people recognize their own inherent faith. It has already started.

5. *Problems*

Authors who can solve them will be sought-after members of society. Even in a smokeless society, where nobody is trying to quit smoking, zillions will still be trying to earn more money, lose weight, attract the opposite sex, make friends, and break bad habits, whatever those habits may be—from addiction to the Internet to addiction to work.

Here and Now

Entrepreneurial Authors won't let their eyes glaze over at the promise of new technology. They will be involved with "here and now" developments more than "distant horizon" developments. They have the patience to wait; they realize that today's technology can propel them to their goals without waiting for somebody's hare-brained (alas, it's often the case) scheme to get off the drawing board.

While some business owners were waiting for computer technology to drop in price, others were making a fortune with the higher-priced older computers. When the new ones were introduced and debugged, The Entrepreneurial Authors had made so much money that they didn't care much about the savings then available.

The past did not list computer literacy or typing ability as skills of a business leader. The present proves that they are musts. The past did not require that you know a second or third language or that you deal gracefully with people from other cultures. The past did not ask you to be interactive, but the future demands it. The Nintendo champ of the year? He used to be a novelty. Now he's the chairman of the board of a Fortune 500 company.

If you are irrevocably bound to the notion of making your company grow large, you're going to have to make it small first. Entrepreneurial Authors may have the goal of market domination, but to achieve it, they must first implement *selective shrinking*. Entrepreneurial Authors view the following dozen areas with an eye toward shrinking them over time. Some of these areas should start out small and stay that way. Others should be reduced slowly over time.

Selective Shrinking

1. Downsize Your Marketing Weapon Arsenal

The process of marketing as an Entrepreneurial Author calls for you to examine and then select a large variety of marketing weapons. Before launching them, you should put them into priority order, then fire them all at once. Your marketing attacks should not be sudden. There's rarely a need to rush, but always a need to plan. Carefully keep track of which weapons are hitting bull's-eyes and which are missing the target. Eliminate the loser techniques. Double up on the winners. The idea is to end up with a small, lethal selection of weapons, every one proved in action.

Small businesses shouldn't try to use all the weapons in their arsenals at once, but should unleash them over time with a well-thought-out plan. Unfortunately, this is a luxury writers don't have. Unless publishers make a commitment to a book, they test-market it with the first printing. To sustain your publisher's belief in your book's future, you have to create maximum promotional firepower for it during the crucial four-to-six-week launch window when it's published.

Firing as many weapons as you can integrate effectively into your plan is the best way to accomplish this. If your book doesn't gain momentum fast enough, your publisher will give up on it and go on to other books.

Make it your goal to use at least sixty weapons. The wider the assortment of weapons you use, the wider the grin on your face will be when your royalty check arrives. However, if you can't use a weapon effectively, don't use it at all.

The more weapons you unleash on publication and the more completely you integrate them, the more powerful each of them becomes. Unity and variety are two of the keys to victory in the publishing wars.

2. Downsize Your Categories of Prospects

Entrepreneurial Authors know well the need to test, and so they do—messages, media, prices, prospects, and a whole lot more. They test a wide range of prospects, using direct marketing and mass marketing. This lets them know which prospects to ignore from now on and which to concentrate upon. Unless they check out a comprehensive selection of prospects, they may miss out on the hottest of all. They want to market like crazy, but *only* to their most torrid prospects. Entrepreneurial Authors have A-lists, indentifying their most rewarding prospects and readers, and they have B-lists, containing the names of those prospects and readers who are less than prime. They focus primarily on that A-list and never hesitate to play favorites.

3. Downsize the Number of Departments in Your Business

If your marketing department is separate from your sales department, there's a chance they'll be marching to different tunes and will be out of step with each other. This is true of all departments. They don't act as cohesively as you'd like; each functions more as a single department than as a whole business. The more they are merged, the more they will understand the common goal and help one another. Simplicity was, is, and will be the byword. Ancient wisdom still holds true: "In the beginner's mind there are many possibilities, but in the expert's mind there are few."

4. Downsize the Number of Key People in Your Company

Business is not a democracy, and although The Entrepreneurial Author is fast to delegate, rarely doing anything herself that can be delegated, The Entrepreneurial Author does not delegate ultimate authority. A business is usually as good as the weakest member of top management. It is clear: only your best should be at the top. You may have many who are good, but very few who are the best.

5. Downsize Your Mission Statement

A narrow focus will be your ally when you create or update your statement of purpose. You did not create your company to do all things for all people, but to do some things for some people with excellence. Employees, readers, customers, prospects, and suppliers should be tuned in to a mission they understand and can help you accomplish.

6. Downsize Your Focus

You may have inaugurated your business with a wide focus, but as you become more experienced and (we hope) wiser, you can adjust that focus and make it smaller. The more acute the focus, the better equipped you will be to succeed, for you will be able to increase your effectiveness and decrease the amount of money used in the past to reach a large target.

7. Downsize Your Niche

The more specialized you niche, the easier it will be to establish it, communicate it, and live up to it. Now that you've been around for a while, perhaps you realize that your niche was too broad. If you can fill a need that no one else fills and occupy a position that is yours alone, your path to success will be smoother.

8. Downsize Your Marketing Plan

The purpose of your marketing may be clearer to you now, and your plan can reflect your enlightenment. The best benefits for you to emphasize are also better known to you than they were at day one. Your target audiences should be smaller in number, your weaponry more selective. Even your budget can be downsized, because you have learned which weapons and tactics to eliminate.

9. Downsize Your Ad Size and Commercial Length

You don't need the impact of large ads as much as the consistency of smaller ads after you've established your business. In ten seconds of video time, you can tell a story that used to take thirty seconds. Your one-minute audio spots can be half that length now. Nearly 80 percent of national TV spots are under thirty seconds in length these days, and it's not the new guys who have that luxury. It's The Entrepreneurial Authors among the behemoths.

10. Downsize the World

That global village you've been hearing about all these years? It's here now. Planet Earth has been shrunk by the Internet far more than by the Concorde, making it more manageable, easier to market to, and not as intimidating. To do business internationally, you need a mouse instead of a passport. As of this moment, 233 nations are connected to the Internet, and you can visit any one of them on your computer monitor. No more jet lag.

11. Downsize the Number of Your Competitors

As you become smarter and conduct your business more effectively, you will save marketing funds while wreaking havoc among your competition. Few will be able to stand up to the withering effects of your enlightened marketing attack. You will have paid the dues of failed experiments and will then reap the benefits of a selective arsenal of weapons. No wonder the competition will fall by the wayside.

12. Downsize the Number of Hours You Are Working

From the start, when you launch your enterprise as an Entrepreneurial Author, and later on when it is running smoothly and profitably, make sure there is balance in your life. You'll probably end up having more energy to devote to your business and a better perspective if you pull back a bit and become involved in something other than your work. It is true that work is noble, but so are you—and you're here on Earth to do more than work hard.

The Omnipotence of Tiny Details

The Entrepreneurial Author makes details list for her enterprise. The list spells out the details that affect her business connections: how the phone is answered, the neatness of the premises, the sincerity of her reader follow-up, and the extra things she does that that give the perception of value at no cost.

A Details List

A details list also goes beyond those Aristotelian senses into the senses of wonder, humor, expectancy, history, health, well-being, security, honesty, and efficiency. You tell the dry cleaner, "It's important that you button these particular buttons on my button-down shirts." Each time, the dry cleaner overlooks the small detail, which is not a small detail to you, or you wouldn't have asked. So it's no surprise when you switch dry cleaners. Tiny details that can undo large efforts exist in any business. Of course, they include customer service, where details are overlooked by the less prepared. Entrepreneurial Authors are aware of the need to save time, so they orient what they do to save time for their readers and clients. Minor details make for major payoffs.

Beyond service, which is obvious, Entrepreneurial Authors have discovered that details can help or hurt you in these ten areas.

Ten Details that will Help or Hurt You

1. *Telephone*

How your telephone is answered and what happens when the person is on hold influence that person's opinion of your business. Entrepreneurial Authors *actively train* anyone who will answer the phone, knowing it is a lifetime to business and that only very special people call. When callers are put on hold, they should hear a recording that gives fascinating information that may prove valuable to them.

2. *Business Card*

What your business card says, what it looks like, and what makes it keepable can make the difference between a customer's occasional patronization and frequent purchases. Business cards have changed. Entrepreneurial Authors give away cards that not only have their address, phone and fax numbers, and e-mail address, but also open up to provide information about their books, offerings, services, and benefits.

3. *Business Hours*

The hours and days you are open and the methods of getting in touch with you make your business either convenient or inconvenient. People expect to be able to contact you when it is *convenient for them.* They want to hook up with your voice mail, e-mail, fax machine, website, or something, and they don't want to wait. Easy to contact means easy to buy from.

4. *Community Work*

The time and hard work that you put *into the community* on an unpaid basis can have a dramatic impact on your business. You might not expect coaching a Little League team to be a business tactic, but your business is part of your life. By giving something to the community, you open wide the conduits through which good things flow into and out of your life.

5. *Cleanliness*

The tidiness of your premises, inside and out—especially the restrooms—is noticed by more people than you may imagine. You might be a bit shocked to know how many people are so put off by messiness that it will keep them forever away from the mess. They really will believe that the messiness pervades your entire organization. Luckily, Entrepreneurial Authors know neatness counts.

6. *Customer Appreciation*

The ability of your salespeople to make readers and prospects feel unique can make the difference between getting one-time customers and all-the-time customers. It is easy for me to tell you this. It will be difficult for you to accomplish but essential if survival—not to mention prosperity—is on your mind. Attention to detail is the key, and research is your guide to detail. Readers must feel that you know what they really are: one of a kind.

One of a Kind

7. *Philanthropy*

Your involvement with a noble cause beyond mere profits will affect people's perception of your business and their desire to do business with you. Align your company with a social cause that will help the planet. Actively work for that cause, and contribute a share of your profits to it. Support organizations or activities that address the problems of the environment, the homeless, AIDS, multiple sclerosis—many causes need your help.

8. *Memory*

Don't forget how you feel when someone remembers your name or your book title. It proves that you mean something to them. It seems like a minor detail, but it happens so infrequently that it's a major detail.

9. Flexibility

A detail everyone will remember and possibly even talk about is how you *veer from your usual practices* and render special service. A Nordstrom department store couldn't deliver a dress to Jay's wife on time, so the salesman offered to deliver it himself. His wife still talks about it and still buys from Nordstrom.

10. Promotional Freebies

Freebies are always appreciated by all demographic, age, and income groups. People expect to pay for things and do not expect to get anything for free. They will long remember your generosity and certainly will remember your name.

WARM RELATIONSHIPS WITH READERS

The People Business

As an Entrepreneurial Author, you must appreciate the underlying truth about what business you are in. You also are in the *people* business, and the more energetically you nod your head while reading this, the better you are at running your business. Entrepreneurial Authors know that warm relationships:

*Come from *consistent follow-up*

*Come from *knowing the reader's name*

*Come from *giving more than is expected*

*Come from *eye contact and smiles*

*Come *individually and not in groups*

*Involve *knowing personal data about people, not merely business data*

*Are created *through caring service*

*Come *when everyone wants them*

*Form the *foundation for future prosperity*

Five Basic Truths

The world-class service lives by five basic truths about customer relationships and how to keep them warm and comfortable:

1. *Make the reader feel unique.* If you do this, you will have established a serious competitive edge over all who would hope to woo your customer from you. If you can make a reader realize that you know what makes him or her unique, you have the potential for a lifetime relationship.

2. *Make the reader feel singled out.* When a reader knows that you have made not a mass-market offer, but a one-of-a-kind offer tailored specifically for the customer, you have struck it rich in your quest for a warm relationship.

3. *Make the reader feel that you want to be of service.* Many companies serve their customers well enough, but seem to be going through the motions. Entrepreneurial Authors see

to it that their employees want to help, honestly care, and render such good service that the reader can actually see they are happy to do so.

4. *Make sure you stay in constant touch with the reader.* The fancy word for this is follow-up, and Entrepreneurial Authors worship at its altar. They stay in touch with readers by phone and mail, with newsletters and direct mail letters. They use their follow-up to make sales. Announce discounts, introduce new items, ask questions via all-important questionnaires, and ask for the names of potential new readers. This follow-up pays itself while providing the added bonus of warming up the relationship through contact.

5. *Make sure you exceed the reader's expectations.* Entrepreneurial Authors are generous, as you have undoubtedly learned, because they see the business rewards of giving. Their generosity also pays off in profits because by giving readers more than they bargained for, The Entrepreneurial Author wins that reader's heart. Exceeding expectations is not the norm. If you exceed them, you will stand out. It is not easy to give that little extra, but try telling that to an Entrepreneurial Author. You'll hear that what's really not easy is staying in business if you can't outperform all competitors.

In order to live by these five basic truths and turn your readers into lifelong customers, you must have the soul of an Entrepreneurial Author. You've got to have the *patience, passion,* and *persistence* of the person who is committed to success. Without these characteristics, it will be difficult to render the kind of service that twenty-first-century readers will demand and expect. Such service is remarkably rare right now, but as the competition heats up and customers gain sophistication, you will be forced, as the price of admission, to provide service that leads readers to want to make *your business* part of *their identity.* That's the payoff of a warm relationship.

Never an Energy Crisis

You must also have *boundless energy,* because knocking yourself out for readers is just what you'll want to do, and you won't be able to do it unless you are fit physically and mentally. Others will wonder where you get your energy, but you'll know that it is generated by your passion for pleasing.

Unless you have a *sense of responsibility,* you might be tempted to leave to others the rendering of warm service. That's great if you can, but you've got to take the ultimate responsibility for the standards of your company's service, for the training of those who might represent you, and for the hiring or forgoing of alliances with these people.

To establish lasting relationships with readers, you must be a *stickler for detail.* Tiny, crucial details do not escape the notice of your customers; they must not be invisible to you. This is especially important in the beginning, when you are generating the momentum that results in superb service. Perhaps later, after the standards are clear to all, you can begin to delegate this vital chore.

You must have *decision-making ability,* because rendering superior service often means making decisions on the spot. Nordstrom, one of the most honored retail chains in history when it comes to customer service, leaves virtually all service decisions to the salesperson. Unless that person is prepared to make a decision at the moment that a decision is needed, somebody is going to be dissatisfied. That's why Nordstrom and *you* must be prepared to decide such matters, despite the risk of being wrong. Entrepreneurial Authors do not pale at the concept of failure.

One final entrepreneurial characteristic necessary to keep readers on your customer list is the *motivation to please.* Unless you are highly motivated to make your customers happy, you're just not going to be able to do it. In fact, if you lack this motivation, you might question whether or not you should be running your own business in the first place. Readers are the reason you are in business; you must aim to please them.

CLOSE RELATIONSHIP WITH YOUR PUBLISHER

Viewing Publishers as Partners

The savvy Entrepreneurial Author views a publisher as a partner, for that in essence is what they are. Each benefits from the actions of the other. Each profits from the excellence of the other.

Once you realize that your publisher is actually your partner in the process, you will want to learn more about that publisher, just as you continue learning about your own enterprise and your audience. The closer you become to the publisher, the more you will gain a "favored nation" status. Old friends do favors for old friends.

To become close to your publisher, you must develop five modes of behavior.

The Care and Feeding of Publishers

1. Stay in Contact

Let your publisher know when they've done something right as well as when they've done something wrong. Keep them up to date on your plans so that they can tailor their plans accordingly, and both of you will avoid crises.

2. Inform Your Publisher of Your Marketing Plan

Give them advance notice so that they can be prepared for an influx of orders. This also lets them know how important you are in the industry and the community so that they will treat your book with the respect it deserves.

3. Be Loyal to Your Publisher

Of course, you will always listen to competitive bids for your work, but deep down, you know that the best relationships are the old relationships, so you see it as your job to improve the publisher's prices, quality, service, or selection with your suggestions rather than deserting them for another. Get your publisher to know your enterprise inside and out so that they develop radar for your needs.

4. Alert Your Publisher to Problems

Let your publisher know if you have a problem. Entrepreneurial Authors do not harbor grudges. Instead, they don't hesitate to pick up the phone (or mouse) to make a call (or send an e-mail) pointing out the problem immediately. Instead of waiting and allowing resentment to build up, solve the problem for yourself and the publisher as quickly as possible. After all, you want this to be a permanent relationship, so get rid of problems as they arise, or they will come back to haunt you.

5. View You Publisher as an Ally

Entrepreneurial Authors know that their publisher might be ideal for a strategic alliance. Your publisher might go in with you on a mutual promotion, a special event, or a publicity effort. Your publisher might even invest in your company, knowing the quality that you offer and how you cherish relationships.

When you have a warm, close, trusting relationship with your publisher, you will receive these benefits:

* Better prices
* Better service
* Availability of product when you need it
* Priority treatment
* Customized handling
* Immediate attention
* In-depth understanding of one another's problems and opportunities
* Kept promises
* Complete honesty
* Advance notice

These are only the surface ways in which you'll benefit. Perhaps the peace of mind of not having to constantly scour for a new publisher will be the biggest benefit of all. And you certainly can't underestimate the power of trust between people.

Authors who have a close relationship with publishers have their fingers on the pulse of their industries. This keen insight provides them with the competitive edge that Entrepreneurial Authors hold so dearly. Every year in the United States, nearly six hundred thousand new books are published. Authors have to seek out publishers and then establish relationships with them once they have learned that they can trust them. Only then can they begin to nurture that relationship to the point at which it can be considered close.

As an Entrepreneurial Author, you'll have the benefit of a close publishing relationship. While your would-be competitors will be out beating the business in search of a trustworthy publisher, you'll probably be at the ballgame with yours. You'll be succeeding at business *and* having a good time—all at once. That's the way of The Entrepreneurial Author.

STRUCTURING YOUR BUSINESS

Structuring Your Business, Entrepreneurial Style

The Entrepreneurial Author structures a business before he has earned one cent, so that as the business grows, it fits neatly into the structure instead of outgrowing it. As the business gets larger, the author does not experience an increase in stress, but rather a decrease, as wisdom replaces trial and error. If you want to structure your business in manner befitting the twenty-first century, this is the framework to use:

1. Structure Your Business to Suit Yourself

Do you think that the Earth revolves around the sun? In a large sense, it certainly does, but in a larger and more cogent sense, it revolves around you. If you're delighted and everyone around you feels the same, you're doing something right. And if you're miserable, spreading misery in your wake, you are undoubtedly doing something wrong. One of the happiest people I know is an auto mechanic who was once a very unhappy lawyer.

The Entrepreneurial Author structures a business around the intensely personal things that make that author a unique individual. You must place yourself above all the components, knowing that you as a person outrank anything about your business.

2. Structure Your Business to Aim for Your Goals

The purpose of your enterprise is to meet its goals. Clearly thought out goals at the outset put you on a track to success. You should be engaged in nothing tangential to your goals—only in activities directed at helping you succeed. Because you have integrated your life with you business, the pursuit of your goals is a healthy endeavor, a price you willingly pay, a foreseen circumstance, and a joy in your life. The perspective of your goals, clarified and illuminated by perfect focus, helps you make many decisions and allows you to visualize what you must do even when your vision may be hazy or temporarily blocked.

That's the big reward when you have a goal. Even if you lose sight of it temporarily, it serves as true north on your entrepreneurial compass and magnetically guides in the right direction.

Go Get Married

3. Structure Your Business to Accommodate Your Family

This may be pretty simple if you have no family, but times change and you very well may have a family later. More than 90 percent of the CEOs of Fortune 500 firms are married. It seems to indicate that marriage and business success can be compatible. Even if you don't get married, you probably have important relationships with parents, siblings, or close friends.

Your business should be structured so that your family stays close to you, remembers your face, enjoys being with you, and does not resent your success. That success should be yours because of them and shared with them, not in spite of them.

All in the Family

Entrepreneurial Authors structure their business so that their family never gets in the way of their work—and vice versa. They do not practice hard-core nepotism, though it is their prerogative.

Instead they are able to engage enthusiastically in their work without knocking over family members in their rush toward the goal line and without leaving cherished relationships in shattered pieces. Because they factored their family into their life and are able to see business as part of their life and not the entire reason for their existence, Entrepreneurial Authors maintain strong family ties, and they are able to love and be loved even though they are succeeding as authors.

1. Structure Your Business to Suit Your Employees

Next to yourself and your family, the people who must want you to succeed in business—and who can do something about it—are your employees. Your business should be structured in a way that gives them room to grow, to flourish, and to prosper as you prosper. Your business structure should provide a fertile ground for your employees to achieve their own goals as you achieve yours. It should balance humanity with capitalism, warmth with effectiveness, and success with sensitivity. The Entrepreneurial Author is a compassionate sort, honestly caring about employees—or independent contractors— almost as though they were members of the author's family. In a sense they are, for they are motivated by similar goals and focused upon the same targets as the author.

Entrepreneurial Authors treat two specific groups with respect, caring, and even reverence. Those groups are their customers and their employees. You already know my feelings about the glory of customers. I feel the same way about employees. No enterprise of an Entrepreneurial Author should be structured in a way that does not reward employees for good work. Each enterprise should have optimum working conditions to promote high morale, employee loyalty, and inclusion in a future edition of *The 100 Best Places to Work in America.* Having worked at one of them, Leo Burnett Advertising in Chicago (and London), I experienced firsthand the bliss of working in an organization that was purposely structured to allow employees to create, produce, and flourish.

2. Structure Your Business to Increase Your Profits

In the century that has now passed, almost all businesses were structured to create profits ahead of everything else—the business owner, family, employees, and even company goals. Profits above all. But that was then. In this enlightened age, profits have a large role, but they are not the proof of success that they used to be. The business of an Entrepreneurial Author is structured, without question, to maximize profits. But the profits grow without any sacrifice of the business author's heart or soul, without exacting heavy payment from family or employees, and without causing a proprietor to sell his soul and be diverted from his goals in pursuit of the hot, flashy buck. The Entrepreneurial

Author is extremely profit-minded, knowing very well the difference between sales and profits.

Pace and Timing

The Entrepreneurial Author also has a sense of pace and timing. This allows her to pursue short-term profits by other avenues. By making the distinction between the short-term and the long run, the author is able to manage a small business while thinking like the owner of a large business. After all, most huge businesses started out as tiny entrepreneurial endeavors.

1. Structure Your Business to Take Advantage of the Technology of Today—and Tomorrow

Entrepreneurial Authors are quite friendly with current technology, not easily wooed by distant technological promises, and disdainful of obsolete technology. That's why in the initial structuring of a business, the author capitalizes on advancements in computers, marketing, communication, and his understanding of the behavioral sciences. Although the life span of technology grows shorter and shorter, and although some technologies thrive for a matter of months before becoming outmoded, Entrepreneurial Authors realize that they are best off embracing what they can use right now—even though it may become old-fashioned in a short time.

They know that by waiting for a computer's price to drop, they are losing money. While waiting for its speed to become faster or its memory larger, they are losing money. They recognize that they are better off riding a horse until the car is invented and then driving the car until the jet plane is invented. In all three cases, they get to their destination faster than if they had walked, and in all instances, they earn more money by using the old technology than by waiting for the prices to drop on the new. Can you imagine existing in today's society as a business without a computer? Millions of businesses are still trying to do just that in effort to save money. These businesses were not structured for existing technology. Their prospects for success are dim.

2. Structure Your Business with Geography in Mind

When Jay structured his first business, he did not factor in geography. So he ended up with a fancy corner office in a Chicago skyscraper, and he pulled in a fancy executive salary. But each winter, his ears nearly froze off on his way to and from that fancy office. And each winter he'd have to fly at least one thousand miles to do the skiing to which he was so addicted. Then, something happened to make him smart. He missed a bus and had to wait thirty minutes in a temperature of minus eighteen degrees. That's when he asked himself, "What am I doing here?" It didn't take long, because he had no adequate answer, for him to restructure his business for geography.

What am I Doing Here?

The point is to ask yourself where you really want to live, and then to become an Entrepreneurial Author *there,* and not where you live now.

Entrepreneurial Authors consider geography when assessing the competitive scene, the size of the job market in case they need employees, and the responsiveness of local government to small business. They factor in the weather, the commute, the overall atmosphere, and the opportunities for doing business globally, for working on their own, and for growth in the first place where they intend to succeed.

1. Structure Your Business to Promote Growth and Diversification

At the beginning, you may want your business to be small and focused on a narrow area. Later you may want to expand or add new products or services. But what if you're structured for expansion or diversity? Tough luck, that's what.

Entrepreneurial Authors' businesses should foresee new economic conditions and the need for growth, so they plan their businesses to fill in niches when niches appear and to solve problems when problems arise. These businesses know they must walk before they run, so they are structured to begin small and then grow or move into other areas. When the expansion takes place, everyone is ready rather than caught off guard. This happy state of affairs occurs because an Entrepreneurial Author structured the business with future growth and diversification in mind. An anonymous business owner once said, "Change occurs only when my back's against the wall." Entrepreneurial Authors, on the other hand, change when they feel like it, and when they are good and ready.

2. Structure Your Business to Maximize Your Passion

You feel glorious about the work you are doing right now. You look forward to work and enter a state of grace while you are doing it. Your passion fuels your fires, which burn intensely hot. That passion becomes translated into enthusiasm as it spreads throughout your company to every one of your employees and then, if you're playing your cards right, to your readers and customers. But perhaps you'll lose your passion. Somehow the fire flickers and goes out. Then what? Do you continue doing the same thing? You'd better *not,* because if you lose your passion, your business will be in a lot of trouble. The fact is that you should seriously consider going into a different line of work. Without passion, you won't succeed at your goal of enjoying your work.

When the Fire Flickers

Entrepreneurial Authors realize that they may lose their current spark and therefore structure their business so that there are other things for them to do—other activities about which they can become passionate. Those activities take place in the very same business. Is it a wild coincidence that they were available? Just the opposite. They are there because the business owner planned it that way. She structured her business so that when burnout took place, a new challenge would arise from the same business.

Never underestimate the power of passion, and never kid yourself as to whether or not you have it. If you burn out on writing, move into speaking. If you burn out on service, move into administration; if you have no more passion for manufacturing, you'll be delighted that you structured your business to let you exercise your passion in another department. A close friend, serving as the president of his own company, found himself burned out completely by the chores of administration. So he turned the reins over to someone else and is now blissfully happy as a salesman. It's not easy to give up the presidency, but for him, it would have been folly to continue in that role.

1. Structure Your Business to Contribute to Your Planet

Three cheers for you, for your family, and for your employees! Now, let's hear a rousing cheer for planet Earth! If the whole world is a bit too large for you, how about your own community? Entrepreneurial Authors know that they are citizens of the Earth and of their community. They exist as individuals, as authors, as members of their family, as part of the community, *and* as part of the whole world. They structure their businesses to let them enjoy all that Entrepreneurial Authors would ever want to enjoy. At the same time, noble causes such as improving the environment, helping the homeless, abetting the U.S. economy, teaching people to read, curing dreaded diseases, and bettering life for children are beneficiaries of their business success as well. The list of causes will continue forever—as will the need for the business community to do something about them.

Perhaps your contribution to these noble causes will come in the form of donating your product or service, making a cash donation, or rolling up your sleeves and volunteering at a soup kitchen. Whatever form your altruism takes, the important thing is to nurture that sense of philanthropy and then activate it with your business. It may sound difficult, but it's actually very easy if you make it part of your overall structure of your business. Whoever heard of creating a small business with the idea of bettering life on Earth? Well, you have now, and Entrepreneurial Authors have been aware of the concept—and even acted on it—for several decades. In the new millennium, giving back to your community or environment will prove to be less a choice for The Entrepreneurial Author, but a criterion for success.

STRUCTURING YOUR TIME

If you're already an Entrepreneurial Author, you don't need to be reminded that time is not money. If time ever was money, it certainly isn't anymore. Time is far more important than money. If you run out of money, there are countless ways to scrounge up more. If you run out of time, it's R.I.P.

Ranked according to what people would do with their time, we learn that:

*15 percent would spend more time with their families

*11 percent would relax

*9 percent would travel

*6 percent would spend time with their hobbies.

*6 percent would work around the house or garden

*6 percent would go back to school to study more

*5 percent would work more

*5 percent would hunt, fish, play golf or tennis, or camp out

*1 percent would read more.

The Benefits of Saving Time for People

Reverence for time is growing rapidly, and Entrepreneurial Authors must be prepared to honor it. Business strategies that save time for people help authors to grow *three times faster* and profit *five times more* than those with strategies that ignore the crucial need for speed. Authors that were aware of time overran their markets, stole the best customers, increased the loyalty of the customers they already had, and became the leading innovators. Better still, their success all but closed off the business to competition. At best, only one or two competitors, moving as rapidly as they could, were able to stay in the game. The rest? Doomed.

Entrepreneurial Authors structure their time according *priorities*. They do not think in terms of nine to five, but instead in terms of accomplishing goals. And they are dramatically different from their counterparts in their ability to *delegate*—to cover their act.

The Word that Everybody Knows

Delegating is a word that everybody knows, but few people practice delegation with skill. Entrepreneurial Authors are masters at passing the buck. To be as adept as they are, to put your delegating money where your delegating mouth is, consider the following ideas:

1. Recognize that every time you delegate successfully, you are doubling your own effectiveness.

2. Unless a task is your passion, don't do it if you can delegate it. Recognize that you are delegating not only work but also responsibility for results.

3. Don't delegate a task to someone who won't do the work as well as—or better than—you can do it.

4. Don't delegate a task to someone if you're not willing to first train that person to do the job with excellence.

5. Don't always tell the person to whom you are delegating *how* to achieve the results. Just talk about the results to encourage initiative.

6. Don't limit the concept of delegating only to work chores; consider it also for the multitude of home chores. Time is time—always precious.

7. When delegating, provide as much information about the task as possible, but don't overload a person with data.

8. When you delegate, be sure that you also delegate the authority to make the necessary related decisions. Let the person to whom you delegate set the terms, timetables, and objectives so he or she can measure how the work is going.

9. Tell the truth about a task to the person to whom you delegate it. If it is drudgery, don't say that the task is glamorous.

10. If you don't know how to trust, you'll have problems delegating. True Entrepreneurial Authors have the ability to trust others with territory and power.

Mastering the art of delegation puts you in control of your time, instead of the reverse. Instead of being dictated by your boss, your clients, your community, and tradition, your time can be governed by different priorities—your own.

Enlightened Selfishness

Structure Your Time Around Yourself

Entrepreneurial Authors know when and how they function best and then arrange their schedule so that they can make their optimum contributions when they are at their peak. They know the importance of energy, vitality, and enthusiasm, and they know they will shortchange their work if they produce the most when they have the least to give. Their entire business plan is designed for *enlightened selfishness*. Peak performance is the result.

Structure Your Time Around Your Goals

Now that you've accommodated your strengths and style in structuring your business, you can devote attention to your skills as an author. Match the operations of your business to your goals as closely as you can. You have honestly clarified your goals. You have been realistic. Structure your time to help you achieve those goals in the most effective manner possible. The way that things used to be done may not be the way they should be done now. Focus on attaining all your objectives.

Structure Your Time Around Your Family or Friends

Your kids' growing up is a one-time performance. There are no encores. The good old days are happening now, and they include a lot more than your financial survival. Youth isn't wasted on the young when the young have their priorities straight and refuse to allow their earning-a-living time to interfere with their living time. Business schools don't encourage entrepreneurs to structure their time to include family and friends, but they will in time. Why should you learn the hard way?

Structure Your Time Around Your Profits

Almost certainly, pursuit of the good old dollar bill will be one of our goals, so when you structure your limited time in this universe, be sure to direct a goodly portion of it toward amassing profits. Those profits may not come instantly, but when you do begin to generate them, they should increase in size every month if you're going about things the right way. That means you're getting wiser every month, learning from mistakes every month, and that your time is well planned. The reality of dealing with people in different time zones, nationally and globally, makes an impact on how you will structure your time. Yet it is possible to have time for yourself, your goals, your friends and family, and still turn a steadily increasing profit. One way is with delegating. The other is with technology.

Technology to the Rescue

Structure Your Time with Technology

In the not-very-distant past, the best time-saver we had was a good grasp of time management—planning, making lists, and prioritizing. That is still an ally of The Entrepreneurial Author, but powerful new forces have joined the battle for time—and the most potent is technology. Technology has presented to time-conscious authors a glorious selection of time-savers. By incorporating this technology into your business *modus operandi* along with the art of delegating, you will be able to structure your time in this evolved way.

Are there really people who can be successful Entrepreneurial Authors while avoiding the traps of "workaholism" and early burnout? Yes, they already exist. Do these people actually succeed while structuring their time according to the guidelines in this chapter? Yes, and success comes to them even more easily because of how they have eliminated unnecessary stress from their lives.

More of those people succeed now than ever before in history. There will be more of them in the next ten years than there are now. These suggestions for structuring your time sound impractical for today's world, but much of today's world is yesterday's world. These suggestions are for tomorrow's world—guideposts that mark The Entrepreneurial Author's way.

Authors playing by the rules of the past run the risk of dying with regrets for things they have not tried.

Now that you are aware of the land of the possible, I hope you don't leave this world regretting that you didn't try your skill by walking the trail of an Entrepreneurial Author.

Being as Flexible
as You Have to Be

Where Entrepreneurial
Authors Are Flexible

Quality was the international byword in the 1980s. In the first ten years of the twenty-first century, it will be *innovation*. Operating in the here and now, Entrepreneurial Authors concentrate upon being the most flexible providers in the land. They already have quality down pat. Of course, they also have several innovative plans for the future. But right now, they are focusing upon flexibility, and they apply it in many areas:

Production Processes

Because innovation will be a hallmark of the future, your production processes will be forced to change in order for you to keep your competitive advantages. Most production process improvements come in the areas of adding speed or economy, so your offerings will have to pass these benefits on to your customers. The only way to do it is to structure your production processes to be flexible. If you don't yet offer an economy-size version of your offering, you'll make changes so that you do.

Shipping Procedures

Because customers are increasingly aware that time is more precious than money, they'll be in a hurry to receive what they just bought from you, be it product or service. Where two-day service was once acceptable, and then upgraded to overnight service by customer demand, same-day service is now the preferred rate of receipt. Thanks to computers and the Internet, same-day service can become "right-now" service. Things that used to be shipped in boxes—books, tapes, DVDs, CDs, and magazines—can now be shipped in bits electronically by computers. Delivery has never been more instant. Entrepreneurial Authors have to be flexible enough to accommodate the public's expectations of speed.

Publisher Relations

Very often, an Entrepreneurial Author can only be as fast as her publisher. The sign of a true Entrepreneurial Author is very fast delivery due to very fast-acting publishers. Entrepreneurial Authors don't maintain business relationships with slow-moving publishers. Instead, they arrange ahead of time for the priority treatment of their account—hence their customers. Entrepreneurial Authors develop such close relationships with their publishers that no deliveries are late and no supplier is tardy. Entrepreneurial Authors deal only with a like-minded publisher who understands the need for speed. What's more, Entrepreneurial Authors may even have entered into a strategic alliance with a publisher. This pays off in closer author-publisher and author-customer relations and more flexibility for The Entrepreneurial Author.

{ CHAPTER 3 }

The Tools

Even Entrepreneurial Authors can't achieve their goals using their bare hands. They need help. They need tools. Some of these tools are in their own minds—such as the ability to focus. Others are living, breathing implements for success in the form of people—employees, independent contractors, or strategic alliance partners. And still others are the authors themselves—or, rather, *first-class versions* of themselves.

One of the most crucial tools is one that you can't see or touch, but it is becoming increasingly valuable with time. It's data, and it's getting easier to get and easier to filter.

Certainly the tools for making it with your own business in the twenty-first century include the tools of technology. The technologies available are becoming more ubiquitous, easier to use, lower in cost, and nearly mandatory. Technologies connect Entrepreneurial Authors with other people, ideas, and things, enabling them to avail themselves of the tool of global unity.

Opportunities that were not even imaginable during most of the twentieth century exist all over the world now because of the collapse of the trade barriers and the creation of the Internet.

THE NEED TO FOCUS

Many authors have no clue as to what they should focus on. Entrepreneurial Authors know there are *three specific areas* upon which their gaze must be narrowly focused:

* *Their own reason for being.* Knowing that writing things down hones their focus, Entrepreneurial Authors prepare a written statement of their purpose. It is in on paper and in their hearts at all times.

* *Their potential target markets.* They want to achieve maximum profitability, and so they carefully select the markets that will help fulfill that goal, realizing they may have multiple targets.

* *Their market niche.* This means focusing on their readers, their prospects, their competitors, and the realities of their marketplace.

What Focus Does

What, exactly, does focus do for an author? It keeps the goals in sight, and those goals are the bright light that illuminates the way for the author. Focus changes "what might be" into "what will be." Many entrepreneurial, freedom-loving types are wandering spirits—free souls carried by chance and opportunity to wherever the winds blow. Entrepreneurial Authors know that goals leave nothing to chance. Goals force you to be specific. And focus keeps the goals in clear view.

You hear daily horror stories of failed businesses, and you wonder how you can succeed while others have fallen by the wayside. The way to do it is to set goals and focus on them. Here's a depressing statistic: *only 2 percent* of the population puts their goals into writing. This number certainly doesn't depress Entrepreneurial Authors. Instead they are encouraged by it, because it indicates the low level of competition out there. Of course businesses are going to fall on their capitalistic faces if they have no written goals.

Never state as a goal something you do not believe in. In order to keep that goal in clear focus, you must believe in your heart that it will happen. You must be able to visualize it. More than one wise Entrepreneurial Author has said, "If you can visualize it, you can will it; and if you can will it, you can achieve it."

If failure to focus is the number one reason for business failure, and if not having goals leads to focus failure, why don't more people set goals in the first place? Terri Lonier, in her terrific book *Working Solo,* gives three reasons.

Why People Don't Set Goals

1. Fear of Embarrassment at Not Reaching Their Goals

Lonier quotes motivational speaker Tony Robbins as saying, "Success comes from good judgment, which comes from experience. But where does experience come from? Bad judgment. The only failure is if you stop. If you quit, you're sure not to succeed."

Everyone who has achieved greatness has experience failure. Thomas Edison failed over forty times. If he was embarrassed at those failures, we might still be groping in the dark. Hockey great Wayne Gretzky said, "You miss 100 percent of the shots you never take." As one who has been of The Entrepreneurial Author variety for some time, I'd say that failure, embarrassment, stumbling, and falling are part of the deal of being an Entrepreneurial Author—and some of the reasons that eventual success tastes so sweet.

2. Fear of Never Being Able to Change Your Goals Once You've Set Them

Although commitment to your goals increases the likelihood of bringing them to happy fruition, those goals belong to you, and you don't belong to them. Often, changing is a foolish thing you do, and brilliant plans are abandoned because of an unnecessary change in goals. But there are occasions when change is prudent. Remember that this section of the book is about *tools*, not about *laws*, and that flexibility is a necessity in an entrepreneurial career. Your goals are your slaves, not your masters. With time and new insight, you probably will alter your goals because you've become smarter. Only with focus will you know if and when to make changes.

3. Fear of Not Having the Ability or Not Being Worthy Enough to Reach Your Goals

One of the main reasons people don't set goals is because of low self-esteem. They underestimate their own power and probably have no inkling of the power of their unconscious minds. Others figure that if they do accomplish their goals, they will be expected to work at that level at all time, something that is not part of their dream. Still more fear the rejection of outsiders who they imagine might be doubting them, thinking, "Who do you think you are?"

The magic ingredients for selecting goals that can be focused upon with ease, as well as attained, are these:

How to Set Goals

1. Set Specific Goals

Don't say "Our business will grow" when you can say "Our business will grow at 20 percent per year for the first five years." Use numbers. Give dates. Set goals that may be broken down into little chunks so that you can move systematically. Remember that a marathon is only a series of connected steps made one at a time. Connect visual images with your goals, because if you can see them, they will be much easier to achieve.

2. *Put Your Goals into Words*

You can focus easily on words that you can read. Although you may know in your heart what your goals are, give your heart the benefit of the brain and your visual sense. Some successful Entrepreneurial Authors think that putting goals on paper is the most important step to attaining them. A famous study of the Yale University class of 1953 revealed that only 3 percent of the class had committed their goals to paper. Twenty years later, subsequent research among the same students showed that the 3 percent had achieved more financial success than the remaining 97 percent of their classmates combined.

3. *Review Your Goals Regularly*

This alone will help you keep your goals in constant focus. Entrepreneurial Authors actually set aside time regularly to review, assess, and evaluate their goals. This keeps them on track, measures their performance, and prevents them from being intimidated by lofty goals. Experts call this "managing your goals"—changing them as you change and as your business changes, ideally keeping their thrust alive.

PEOPLE—THE LIFE FOCUS OF ANY BUSINESS

No Bad Employees, No Bad Attitudes

In an ideal organization run by an Entrepreneurial Author, there are no bad employees, no bad attitudes, no lack of training, no self-consciousness at the repetition necessary for proper training, and no hints of amateurism anywhere in their firms. If an employee makes a mistake, he makes it only once. This efficiency will be more valuable than ever.

Ten Traits to Look For

If you had to pick ten traits to look for in anyone with whom you connect, these would be the ones to go for:

1. A dedication to the achievement of your company's goals
2. A pleasant personality that is compatible with yours
3. A fearlessness to learn—especially new technologies
4. A desire to improve, manifested by constant learning
5. An optimism that doesn't burn out
6. An abundant level of physical and mental energy
7. A well-organized life, on and off the job

8. The capacity for enthusiasm that grows to passion

9. A balance in life that makes the person burnout-proof

10. The ability to write and to type

DUPLICATE YOURSELF
AND YOUR TOP PEOPLE

Entrepreneurial Authors have a trick up their sleeves. It allows them to increase their effectiveness, their time, and their freedom. If they do it right, their businesses can continue to generate profits even after the authors have stopped working. This trick is the *ability to duplicate themselves,* to hire and train employees who can make some or all of their entrepreneurial instincts.

Ten Hints to Help You

In finding people to serve as your own duplicates, here are ten hints that will help you delegate with confidence:

1. Look for people who have *track records.* It's all well and good if a prospective clone is skilled, trained, and says the right things; but if they've actually done what you want them to do for you, and if they've done it well, they should have an inside track in the duplication sweepstakes.

2. Do your *own personnel research.* If there's any data you do *not* want to receive secondhand or by hearsay, find it

yourself. Such a matter should not come to you through a filter, but through your own eyes, ears, and observation.

3. Duplicate yourself with *ordinary people,* but train them for *extraordinary results.* Your duplicates can achieve the extraordinary with the right training, the right attitude, the right level of enthusiasm, and by good example. Still— don't clone a mouse to do an elephant's work.

4. Realize that delegating is the *cheapest form of manufacturing.* Entrepreneurial Authors don't want to build a factory when they can use somebody else's. They know of a quote, quite famous and popular in Italy: "I wish you many employees." You're in business for profit, not power.

5. Try to duplicate yourself through *someone who knows more than you do.* Entrepreneurial Authors do not feel challenged by a bright employee who might eclipse them. They know that such a duplicate will help grow a business just as long as the person is on the same business wavelength as they are.

6. On the other hand, *someone who is smarter than you* is not necessarily a good duplicate. You have to take many strengths other than your I.Q. into consideration. A good track record is better than a great academic record. A pleasant duplicate may be better than a perfectionist duplicate.

7. Look among *your existing employees* to find a potential duplicate. Most employees want to know they can advance to bigger and better positions, so look within to find those who best understand you, your goals, and your business. This helps your business and their morale.

8. Duplicate yourself through people who are *willing to work hard.* The Entrepreneurial Author avoids being a workaholic but does not avoid work. The author loves work, handles it with passion, and keeps it in balance. Never let pure talent blind you to the need for a hard worker.

9. Creating a duplicate Entrepreneurial Author is like *getting married.* Think of the long haul. Take great care. Plan to respect and trust your duplicate. Remember that if it doesn't work out, divorces can be painful and costly.

10. Duplicate yourself through a person who is *not afraid to make decisions.* The inability to make decisions can destroy a company. Your duplicate must be as much of a risk-taker as you are. Indecisiveness paralyzes business; the window of opportunity does not remain open indefinitely. If you don't act, your competitor will. The Entrepreneurial Author would rather make a wrong decision than no decision. Be sure those to whom you delegate work recognize this.

DATA—THE CURRENCY
OF THE TWENTY-FIRST CENTURY

The two main social classes in the twentieth century were the *rich* and the *poor*. The two main social classes in the twenty-first century are the *informed* and the *clueless*.

Information will be The Entrepreneurial Author's ticket to success as well as to:

*Happiness

*Wealth

*Power

*Love

*Health

*Longevity

*Security

*Freedom

*Time

*Enlightenment

If you were allowed into a vault filled with $100 bills, $50 bills, $20 bills, $10 bills, $5 bills, $1 bills, and pennies, you would know exactly which currency you'd want to take. It would be a simple decision, rapidly made; you'd take the $100 bills. If the vault was filled with information, clearly labeled, you might not know which pieces you should take. You simply wouldn't recognize the value of each. The crisp green bills might be worth less than the dulled pennies.

Which Information to Access

Unless you know which information you *need*, you may operate your life and your business based on useless information. To avoid this, Entrepreneurial Authors seek a *data filter*. They're keenly aware that data is crucial for the care and feeding of current readers, for the obtaining of new customers, and for outpacing the competition—which is no slouch when it comes to getting information. Simplified technology and burgeoning data banks offer oceans of data to those who seek it.

Intimacy with the Internet

New generations, raised on Nintendo and video arcades, now use the Internet as their primary source of data. Intimacy with the Internet is your ticket to ride first class in the information age. Point, click, and be informed quickly.

Broadcatching

Entrepreneurial Authors wake up, walk into their office, switch on their computers, and see a message startlingly similar to this one: "Hi. I read 24,394 new stories from around the world this morning. Here are the five you will most want to read." That's what I mean by data filter. The technology is here right now and has been for several years. Some information hounds refer to it as "broadcatching."

The Information You Want

As an Entrepreneurial Author, you'll jump on that information lighting fast, much faster than the behemoths that are your competition. And just what kind of information will you be after?

> *Reports and statistics* that help you understand markets
>
> *Customer contacts* that expand your customer list
>
> *Supplier contacts* that help you lower your costs
>
> *Inside intelligence* and insights about your competitors and yourself
>
> *Professional advice* about any aspect of your business

What You Won't Find on the Internet

But don't end your information search with you forays onto the Internet. True, it's a big library, but there's a lot of data it does not provide, and when information is currency, you want all the data you can get. Some of the information you'll want and may not find online includes:

> *Information about your *own product or service*—the more, the better
>
> *Information about *your readers*—get as much as possible

*Information about your *competitive advantages,* which you
find or create

*Information about your *competitors,* gleaned only by
personal effort

*Information about *potential marketing partners* or
strategic alliances

In the information age, The Entrepreneurial Author collects
data on and off the Internet, with and without a computer, always
blending hard, cold information with human observation and
understanding, and never viewing the technology as a master but
only as a guide.

MODULAR PROFIT ALLIANCES

Entrepreneurial Authors have known all along to search for
others with whom to cooperate rather than compete. It's nice
that the world is catching up. The whole idea is to create or
hook up with an existing profit alliance. The sole purpose of the
alliance is *mutual profit,* and the alliances are temporary, never
permanent. They will provide you with prosperity—with a little
help from your friends. And you have more friends than you
may realize. Consider those with whom you might enter into a
profit alliance.

Potential Alliance Partners

Competitors from far away. They probably know what works and what doesn't work in their neck of the woods, and they'll gladly share knowledge with you if you have knowledge to share with them.

Competitors from nearby. They'll see the good sense of sharing the potential rather than battling for it, and they'll like the idea of reducing their marketing costs.

Publishers. They know that as you grow, they'll grow too, and they know that you're good at what you do, because they've been working with you for a while and keeping an eye on you.

Fellow Entrepreneurial Authors. They've learned that being part of a loose-knit network is a lot better than being out there all alone, and maybe they have the same kind of prospects and customers that you do.

Investors. They'll love the thought of getting rich by your brains, time, and toil, and you've convinced them that your business will succeed, helping them succeed in turn.

Lenders. There is a strong rationale for any bank or other lending institution to help a company it has deemed worthy of a loan.

Employees. This will make them feel more a part of management, will foster their proprietary and spirit, and will ensure their emotional connection—a bonus for both of you.

Landlords. You have proved yourself a desirable tenant who is capable of growing a business, and the landlord knows that profitability reflects reliability—a valued asset in a renter.

The community. Your success will enrich it by providing economic stability and by attracting capital and possibly even employment opportunities.

Online neighbors. They are part of your digital neighborhood and they know you, have witnessed your growth, and might see you as an opportunity to increase their Internet presence as well as their global reach.

Entrepreneurial Authors view *all* other authors as potential partners, as allies, and as possible parts of a network that can help in many ways. They realize that consistent success and growth in the twenty-first century will be a hallmark of teams and not single players.

When you open your mind to the idea of connecting with others for the goal of profitability all around—for an alliance might consist of two or fifteen—be aware of what you have to offer, what you need, and what your potential partners have to offer and need. You can help each other in at least ten areas:

1. Planning
2. Technology
3. Inventory
4. Management
5. Human beings
6. Customer service
7. Work space
8. Purchasing power
9. Marketing
10. Information sharing

Generally, profit alliances are best entered into by enterprises that have *the same kind of customers.* This way each one can refer the customer to another member of the network—all in the best interests of the customer. Although I urge you to enter into alliances with the goal of profitability, your bottom-line goal should be *the good of the customer.* If it is, you'll be better at spotting such alliance possibilities. You'll know that by entering into them, you'll be able to provide better service.

You are in business at the cresting of the wave of working from home and being an entrepreneur, so you get to set the rules of the game to fit your own tastes. Although Thomas Edison formed a dynamite profit alliance with Corning Glass a long time ago, resulting in the light bulb—electrical filaments by Edison, glass by Corning—the concept of such teaming up is still relatively new. So you can create and mold your alliances any way you see fit.

{ CHAPTER 4 }

The Secrets

To many, the secrets of succeeding in the life of an Entrepreneurial Author aren't really secrets at all, but plain and simple common sense. But because common sense is so uncommon these days, you'd think it is a secret, for so many authors lack it.

It should be no secret that the key to survival and prosperity is proper management. If everything is in order except the management, expect dire results. If you don't realize that behind all the complexities of business are human beings, you will be lost in the capitalistic wilderness. If changes throw you for a loop and you haven't prepared for them, you should be minding someone else's business and not your own, taking orders instead of giving them.

The way of an Entrepreneurial Author involves combining the best of the past with the best of the present. The idea of convenience is not very new, but the concept of moving beyond convenience is so novel, most authors don't have a clue what is means. It means being the most convenient, the fastest, the simplest to buy from, and giving more than is expected.

MANAGING IN THE NEW REALITY

The number-one cause of business failure in the United States and elsewhere is *poor management.* What are the traits of good management?

The Traits of Good Management

1. *The ability to focus*—never losing sight of the goal of the business
2. *The ability to lead,* which means to inspire effectiveness
3. *The ability to relate* to employees, partners, readers, customers, and suppliers
4. *The ability to change*—static leadership is doomed from the start
5. *The ability to reflect*—seeing the whole picture

Don't Give Readers What They Expect

Do Entrepreneurial Authors give readers absolutely everything they expect? Of course not. Anyone can do that. Entrepreneurial Authors manage by giving readers the unexpected—which is *more* than they anticipated, *better* than they anticipated, *faster* than they anticipated, *more convenient* than they anticipated, and *offered with better service* than they anticipated.

Top authors are now playing by three new rules:

1. Excellence in One Dimension

Provide the best offering in the marketplace by excelling in a specific dimension of value. Great management does not try to excel in all of these, because it's right at the border of the impossible. They do try to be the best in one of them.

2. High Standards

Maintain threshold standards on the other dimensions of value. Just because you're proficient at one thing doesn't mean you can ignore the others.

3. Improved Value

Dominate your market by improving your value every year. You can be sure that if you're doing enough to be a leader, your competitors will be paying close attention, so you've got to continue getting better all the time. That's what your readers are hoping for. Entrepreneurial Authors strive to constantly deliver the best performance in their selected dimension of value.

You will soon learn—if you haven't already—that managing means taking responsibility. As in golf, where you have only yourself to blame or praise, and unlike the team sports, management is a game in which you are really the person in whom resides *sole responsibility.* When a football team draws a lot of penalties, I blame the coach for lack of good and disciplined instruction. When they make several miracle plays in the fourth quarter to win the game, I give the credit to the coach. Other players may have made the mistakes or the big plays, and yet it is the person who made it happen—or not happen. *Somebody* has to be in charge. And in a business that somebody is the management—you.

The best managers have to deal with many emotions, and at the same time accomplish these goals:

*They inspire people to perform above their capabilities.

*They create confidence among their customers and employees.

*They are obsessed with quality.

*They have the intestinal fortitude to get the job done—no matter what.

*They have an equal blend of heart and brains. They also have soul.

*They lead by example.

*They willingly take responsibility for everything.

*They accept neither praise nor money if it is not deserved.

*They are honest with themselves and with others.

*They love people.

Good managers love people. They are also aggressive. This is because they are oriented to results. They don't mind bruising an ego or two, but they mean nothing personal by it, because their assertiveness is always directed at ideas and not at people. They are fully aware that an aggressive spirit—an entrepreneurial trait if ever there was one—is a necessary catalyst in the chemistry of motivation.

SELLING WITH THE SECRETS OF HUMAN BEHAVIOR

People, but with Emotion

The Entrepreneurial Author is not surprised to find that people often make purchases primarily because of emotion. You might think that it's because of rational behavior, but that's just not true. People buy with emotion and then justify their purchase with logic. Left-brained people's lives are ruled by logical, sequential reasoning. You'd figure they would make purchases based upon logic, but they don't. When it comes to buying things, they're a lot like the right-brained people who are guided by emotional, instinctive reactions.

The Five "Nevers"

As Entrepreneurial Authors strive to learn the secrets of human behavior, they discover the five "nevers":

1. *Never make a reader feel inferior.* Readers, like you, love to feel smart. How smart? Just as smart as they think they are.

If you undermine this feeling, you're undermining your own efforts.

2. *Never try to impress a reader with industry jargon.* You can use that jargon around the office, with co-workers, and even employees, but never readers. Impress your readers with the benefits that your product or service offers them.

Once the reader becomes a customer, keep them for life with these last three "nevers":

3. *Never take existing customers for granted.* They are worth six times as much to you as a new customer, because it costs one-sixth as much to sell to them. Entrepreneurial Authors fervently practice customer reverence.

4. *Never compete with the customer.* It is a game you will lose even if you think you've won. Do you want to win or to sell? You are dealing with customers to help them, not to beat their pants off.

5. *Never try to win an argument with the customer.* Better still, never engage in such an argument, or you'll win the argument and lose the sale. Remember that there are two Entrepreneurial Author rules about dealing with customers: first, the customer is always right; and second, if you think the customer is wrong, refer back to the first rule.

Three Hard Things

There's only one person you should know better than you know your readers. The job of Entrepreneurial Authors is to *know themselves,* though Benjamin Franklin warned us that "there are three things that are very hard: diamonds, steel, and knowing yourself." By knowing yourself, you can know others without imposing your personality upon them; instead, you *merge* with them in a manner that is comfortable, honest, and mutually effective. To maximize sales effectiveness in the ever-competitive twenty-first century, Entrepreneurial Authors must be able to deal with all personality types—regardless of their own personality.

The way of The Entrepreneurial Author is directed at the needs, wants, and inner workings of people—yourself included. The more you realize this, the more your life as an Entrepreneurial Author will be financially and emotionally gratifying.

BEING PREPARED FOR CHANGE

The Entrepreneurial Author sees how these changes might have an impact on her business. She knows the crucial importance of recognizing *when* she needs to change and *what* to change at that time. She knows she must manage and implement the changes.

The Surfer's Rules

Robert J. Kriegel, in his delightful book *If It Ain't Broke ... Break It!* compares change with surfing on the ocean and offers to entrepreneurs the Surfer's Rules:

- *Passion rules.* The best surfers don't spend lots of time on the beach talking about surfing. They love the water and are out there looking for a wave. They are totally committed surfing in body, mind, and spirit. Some have bumper stickers that say "passion rules." Entrepreneurial Authors might sport the same sticker.

- *No dare, no flair.* Top surfers are constantly pushing their limits, trying new moves, and going for bigger waves, longer rides, and more control. This also means taking risks, constantly challenging yourself and those around you, and improving everyone in the process. Entrepreneurial Authors are famed for both their dare and their flair.

- *Expect to wipe out.* Entrepreneurial Authors know that failed experiments are part of the game, just as surfers know that wipeouts occur about two or three times more often than great rides. The idea is to learn from the wipeouts and realize that if you play it too safe, you won't keep improving.

- *Don't turn your back on the ocean.* The uncertainty and unpredictability of change is exactly the same as that connected with ocean waves. Surfers respect those waves and never take them for granted. Even the world's best surfer can be drowned by a wave or eaten by a shark if he's not paying close attention. *Pay attention.*

- *Keep looking at the horizon.* Just because the wave coming next is a big one and can give you a big ride, notice what is coming after it. Change might be bringing in a wave that can give you the ride of a lifetime or one that can send you crashing down into the sand. Entrepreneurial Authors keep their eyes open and look in all directions.

- *Move before it moves you.* To catch a wave, you've got to begin moving before it comes to you. If you want too long, it will pass you by and leave you in the backwash. Authors who wait too long before speeding onto the information superhighway may become roadkill.

- *Never surf alone.* Surfers know it's important to have the security of a good backup should an emergency arise. They know that by pooling their knowledge and resources with others, they can get the most from their passion. Surfers, like Entrepreneurial Authors, get a little help from their friends.

Change-Killers

All change is not unstoppable. It is possible to stop some change within your own enterprise. It happens every day because of the corporate penchant for change-killers. Change-killers leap up and block change. Here are ten common examples of change-killing statements:

1. It's not in the budget.
2. Nobody here can do the extra work to get it going.
3. It's going to decrease our quarterly numbers.
4. It'll never work.
5. Nobody does it like that now.
6. It's not practical.
7. Things are working the way they are.
8. We've never tried anything like that before.
9. That's never been approved.
10. That's not the way we do things around here.

These statements may not ultimately stop change, but they stop companies from changing—even when change is mandatory. Change-killers are not only unhealthy, but they're also lethal. Companies that never change don't do nearly as well as those that always change. Sure, there should be some natural resistance to change, to weigh its merit and to avoid following fads; change should never get in the way of the primary commitment of The Entrepreneurial Author's operation. A change worth making should simplify the attainment of your goals.

That word *balance* keeps springing up for Entrepreneurial Authors: Balance between work and leisure. Balance between doing and delegating. Balance between changing and keeping things the same. Remember that balance incorporates two or more items rather than one. Too many changes are as ill-advised as no changes. The Entrepreneurial Author accepts change as part of life and instead of resisting or ignoring it, uses it to move forward—the favorite direction of all Entrepreneurial Authors.

MARKETING WITH THE TWENTY-FIRST-CENTURY WEAPONS

It is interesting to note that the difference between marketing in the twentieth century and marketing in the twenty-first century is almost identical to differences between old-fashioned marketing and marketing as an Entrepreneurial Author.

MONEY

- Twentieth-century marketing mandated that you *invest money* in order to do a good job at marketing your business.
- Twenty-first-century marketing mandates that you *invest time, energy,* and *imagination* in marketing your business.

MARKETING DECISIONS

- Twentieth-century marketing decisions were based on *judgment, intuition,* and *guesswork,* and rarely upon science.
- Twenty-first-century marketing decisions are based as much as possible upon *psychology,* the emerging science of human behavior.

MEASURING STICKS

- Twentieth century marketing measured the effectiveness of its weapons by *sales, turnovers, traffic, response rate, cost per order,* and *volume.*
- Twenty-first century marketing measures the effectiveness of its weapon by one yardstick—*profits*—the dear old bottom line.

SIZE OF BUSINESS

- Twentieth century marketing was geared to *ultra-large businesses* with limitless marketing budgets.
- Twenty-first century marketing is geared to *small businesses*—and to start-ups and hoe-based businesses with *limited marketing budgets.*

NEW VS. EXISTING CUSTOMERS

- Twentieth century marketing is oriented to *making the sale* and then *going on to look for new customers.*
- Twenty-first century marketing is oriented to *making the sale* and then *practicing fervent devotion to follow-up with existing customers.*

MARKETING MYSTIQUE

- Twentieth-century marketing *enshrouded marketing in a cloak of mystique,* causing many authors to be intimidated by it.

- Twenty-first-century marketing removes the cloak, *eliminates the mystique* from marketing, and allows authors to feel in control of it, to understand it, to feel no sense of intimidation by it.

COMPETITION VS. COOPERATION

- Twentieth-century marketing is based upon *competition,* finding butts to kick, heads to pound, businesses to pulverize.

- Twenty-first-century marketing is based upon *cooperation,* finding businesses of all types with which to form strategic alliances for mutual profit.

SALES VS. RELATIONSHIPS

- Twentieth-century marketing aims at making *sales,* for sales are the key to the kingdom.

- Twenty-first-century marketing aims at making *relationships* because one-time sales only lead to a temporary high.

MARKETING COMBINATIONS

- Twentieth-century marketing mistakenly believes that *advertising works* when it doesn't and that direct mail works when it doesn't.

- Twenty-first-century marketing correctly believes that advertising doesn't work and direct mail doesn't work, but that *only marketing combinations work,* and that when you combine advertising with direct mail, they both work.

MARKETING WEAPONS

- Twentieth-century marketing features *five or ten marketing weapons* and urges business owners to use two or three of them.

- Twenty-first-century marketing features *at least one hundred marketing weapons,* half of them free, and many of them available only if you're online. The idea is to use many and then cut that number down based on results. Sixty is ideal.

The Ten Best Marketing Weapons

Of the hundred weapons available to you, ten are the most important. Ten should be illuminated forever by a neon sign in your brain; you should incorporate them into your entrepreneurial DNA. Can you make do with only nine of these? You can, but if you have even the vaguest interest in money, you'll probably want to utilize all ten:

1. *Marketing Plan*

    Not having one is like entering battle under a commander whose only advice is "Ready! Fire! ... Aim!" You aren't going to win many battles that way, yet that's the way many are waged. Not yours, though. Your marketing plan has to be only seven sentences long—describing your purpose, primary benefit and competitive advantage, target audiences, marketing weapons, niche, identity, and budget. Don't even think of waging a battle or producing marketing materials without a plan.

2. Passion

You've just got to feel passion, not only for your business and the benefits it provides, but also for the marketing process, the research you must do, your computers, your fellow networkers, and your opportunities. If you don't honestly feel that passion, you're going to have a lot of trouble generating the enthusiasm your customers and co-workers will feed on. If you don't feel a burning passion, you seriously should consider another line of work.

3. Benefits List

Prepare a written list of the benefits of doing business with you. Those benefits will help you market what you wish to sell. Put a circle around those benefits that are true competitive advantages, for they will become your marketing superstars, the places where those who create your marketing will hang their hats. The longer your benefits list, the more ammunition you will have to win the battle for the customer. Your benefits list is more valuable than money, yet money can't buy it.

4. *Community Involvement*

People would much rather buy from friends than strangers, and by making yourself part of the community, you remove yourself from the ranks of strangers. Community involvement really means working so hard for the community on a volunteer basis that people are dazzled by your conscientiousness. Your hard work for your community transcends any words you might put into a brochure or ad, proving beyond a doubt that yours is a business worth patronizing.

5. *Fusion Marketing*

This extraordinary weapon is certainly not a new one. You can be sure the Minnesota farmers had it in mind when a group of people then figured that they might get together on marketing their veggies under the name "Green Giant." Fusion marketing has been called *tie-ins, collaborative marketing,* and *co-marketing.* It's based upon a simple idea: "If you scratch my back, I'll scratch yours." And it means Entrepreneurial Authors can increase their marketing exposure without upping their marketing investment. The more you try this weapon, the more you'll thank me for suggesting it. But don't thank me. Thank the big jolly guy in his valley.

Never Love 'Em and Leave 'Em

6. Follow-Up

Nearly 70 percent of customers lost to American businesses are lost because of apathy after the sale—the seller's "love 'em and leave 'em" attitude. The opposite of apathy is follow-up. Many business owners, destined to fail at their businesses, think that marketing ends once they've made the sale. True-blue Entrepreneurial Authors know that at the sale, real marketing *begins*. They know that few businesses practice sincere follow-up regularly and reverently. They are keenly aware that it costs six times more to sell something to a new customer than to an existing customer, and they experience the beauty and economy of referral business. If you ask a golfer the name of the game, the golfer will say, "Putting." If you ask an Entrepreneurial Author the name of the game, the author will say, "Follow-up." And those people are *professionals*.

7. Customer Research

You know by now that information is the currency of the twenty-first century. Of all the data in the universe—covering your marketing, your competition, your media options, your industry, and your locale—by far the most important to you is the data about *your customers*. Where to get it? By asking the customers themselves via questionnaires, in person, or any way you can. Data is money. Customers have the data. They will happily give it to you if you only ask for it. So ask for it—early and often.

8. *Online Presence*

The first seven weapons of the twenty-first century were alive and kicking in the twentieth century. This one was an infant. But with media fragmenting into special interest magazines, zone area newspapers, regional edition publications, cable and satellite television, selected format radio, and targeted direct mailings, where does everything come together? *Online and right at your Web site*—on the Internet. All your marketing will eventually pay off at your Web site. The World Wide Web is still a baby, but it's a baby that you want to have as a very close friend.

9. *The Designated Guerrilla*

Every twenty-first-century business will need one, and if it's not you—because you lack the time or the passion for solid Entrepreneurial Authorship—it should either be someone from within your organization who just loves the idea of riding the herd over a superabundance of marketing weapons or someone from the outside who feels the same way and understands your mindset. The whole purpose of marketing as a Guerrilla is action. These weapons are meaningless without the infusion of action provided by your designated Guerrilla. This book may be opening the door for you, but it's up to you to walk through the doorway.

The Entrepreneurial Author's Credo

10. Satisfied Customers

Every person you have satisfied in the past is another weapon in your arsenal, another name for your mailing list, another source of repeat business, and another person who will refer others to you. Satisfied customers are the wondrous spring from which flow testimonial letters, success stories, referral business, and before-and-after tales. Best of all, this marketing weapon doesn't cost anything. It actually pays.

Selecting Your Niche

As you read this, the market is busily splintering into fragments. Entrepreneurial Authors have a name for these fragments. They call them niches. They know that niches are becoming smaller and smaller and that if they select the right niche, they may be more than halfway home already As niches grow smaller, customers grow more important- and they know it, so you'd better be prepared to give them the treatment they deserve.

You'd better be prepared to "narrowcast" instead of broadcast, to do micromarkcting instead of mass marketing, and to reach inward toward customers more than outward toward prospects. Entrepreneurial Authors are gloriously positioned to capitalize on niche marketing. They're able to differentiate themselves in ways important to their prospects and customers. They're able to get rolling on that information and communications highway in a way that little guys couldn't in the mid-twentieth century. Now everyone can afford a computer and online service. Is this the price of admission to the future? You know it is. Does that mean technology will outweigh the human touch? Just the opposite. Personal selling will be more important than ever, and online communication will add the personal element. People today buy from those they trust. People tomorrow will do the same. The two forces that govern sales will be *advanced technology* and *personal service*. Combining them, Entrepreneurial Authors will thrive as never before.

Enjoying the process of marketing and then using it to its greatest advantage are without question essential to the way of The Entrepreneurial Author.

GETTING INTERACTIVE

What's the first thing to enter your mind when you read the word *interactive*? Most authors think first of technology. Entrepreneurial Authors think first of people. They know that *interactive* means "to act reciprocally," rather than to act technologically. Being interactive means being connected, giving and taking, and responding.

Connections that promote interactively take place in person, by phone, by mail, and online. That means that Entrepreneurial Authors are interactive in a multitude of forums.

The Many Ways of Being Interactive

The traditional *live event* is probably the most widespread method of conducting business interactively. Zero technology is required. Maximum psychological savvy helps. Entrepreneurial Authors relish the eye contact, the warm handshake, and the smell of ink drying on the dotted line. They may not even own a computer, but are classic examples of being interactive.

An Entrepreneurial Author's *involvement with the community* is also a form of interactivity. In this case, the interaction is first with a group and then with individuals. A truly interactive Entrepreneurial Author is a member of several community organizations, contributing to the betterment of the local scene as well as being in a position to do some powerful *networking*—still another form of interactivity.

Brochures, electronic and printed, are interactive tools because they are requested or mailed; then they provide information before asking for action—usually a purchase. And to promote interactivity, they frequently offer a coupon, a toll-free phone number, or an e-mail address. Interactivity doesn't always require a lot of back-and-forth communication, as you would experience in face-to-face meetings and phone calls (the ultimate in interactivity). To be interactive, someone acts and someone else reacts. The amount of acting and reacting is irrelevant. Getting the desired action is all that counts.

Entrepreneurial Authors who realize that interactivity leads to lasting relationships with readers are also hitting the interactive trail when they offer *free consultations,* a potent marketing weapon if ever there was one, with *free seminars* that invite questions and are set up to close sales, and with *speakers who talk to groups* for free and then distribute brochures and establish relationships.

Whatever You Read, Wherever You Look

Another influence on an Entrepreneurial Author's behavior is the Internet. Whatever people read, wherever they look, they keep learning about the Internet. There are several ways that guerrilla entrepreneurs conduct, market, and transact their business online.

Being interactive means not only giving information, but also seeking information. The Internet allows you to engage in market research—and accomplish this for hardly any investment in an age when information is king.

Disaster Avoidance

Informal focus groups on the Internet that include the appropriate people will let you know whether your products or services have flaws or good potential. You can get honest feedback from people just like your prospects. Entrepreneurial Authors use this capability as disaster avoidance. They make valuable use of the Internet by exploring these focus groups, by perusing the wealth of reference material available, and by subscribing to electronic clipping services.

The Internet is the fastest-growing method of being interactive. Remember that no matter how large it gets, it will always be about people, will always boil down to one-on-one transactions, and will never replace face-to-face contact. The Internet is faster, more convenient, and far more economical than mass media in reaching large numbers of people. But you should never consider your business to be interactive strictly because you subscribe to an online service or have your own.

How do you answer your phone? If you don't make all callers feel good that they called you, you're dropping the interactive ball. If you keep them on hold without informing or entertaining them, you're falling on your interactive keister. If you don't look them in the eye when you talk to them in person, you're not giving interactivity all that you should. If you know about their personal lives, you're missing out on the most important aspect of interactivity—relating, human to human, as closely and warmly as possible.

AVOIDING BECOMING A WORKAHOLIC AND STRESS

A life dedicated primarily to working and amassing a fortune is only part of a life if friends, family, fun, recreation, and relaxation are left in the dust. Entrepreneurial Authors are much more than earning machines. Almost anyone focused on money will get it if they put in enough time and effort. Achieving serenity and balance is more difficult. There are fewer role models for this lifestyle. The newspapers list only the one hundred wealthiest people in the world, not the one hundred happiest.

Four Important Things

To get your name on the list of the one hundred happiest people, there are four very important things you need to know:

1. Succeeding in your own business means that you must constantly work *more than forty hours a week, weekends, and evenings.*

2. Running your own enterprise carries with it the realization that the responsibilities *will cause stress*—sometimes lethal.

3. There *really is a Santa Claus,* and his sleigh is pulled through the sky by reindeer every Christmas Eve.

4. *The Easter Bunny exists all year long* and spends all of his time as an egg-painting workaholic.

File those un-facts away where you keep your tales by the Brothers Grimm and your poems by Mother Goose. They are widely believed, but they simply aren't true. The true workaholics are those who choose work over any other method of spending time—a woeful condition. They fail to plan ahead and incorporate balance into their lives, they lose control of situations to extraneous circumstances, they spend time putting out fires instead of generating profits, and they have misguided priorities and operate according to early-twentieth-century dictates.

You often read of the problems caused by the abuse of alcohol and the depressingly high number of people who die of alcoholism. But you don't see much about abuse of work and the fact that more workaholics are dying faster and younger than alcoholics, that the affliction called "karoshi syndrome" (death from overwork) is now the number two cause of death in Japan.

Diane Fassel, author of *Working Ourselves to Death,* was interviewed by the *San Francisco Chronicle.* She said,

> A group of insurance agencies asked me to investigate a trend they couldn't understand. They were getting a surprisingly high number of claims for 30-day in-patient drug and alcohol treatment of children of employees. I found that the parents of these kids were workaholics—their life was unmanageable, they were obsessed with business and deadlines and success. Their kids were in quite a bit of emotional pain from the lack of connection they felt toward their parents and had begun acting out with drugs and alcohol. The irony was that the kids were going to treatment while the parents, who were addicts, remained untreated. That was because in the adults, addiction wasn't seen as real; it appeared to be a normal way of life.

Fassel's book says that being a workaholic is socially promoted because it is seemingly socially productive; but the truth, according to her, is that workaholics end up costing companies money because they produce in spurts. Rush-aholic work addicts look busy, but they are usually moving so fast that they make mistakes.

Workaholics are Losers

Along with robbing you of time, abuse of work by overwork leads to stress, causes you and others to make mistakes, and penalizes your customers with shoddy service—and therefore has a negative impact on quality. The Entrepreneurial Author does not have a wealth of experience with six-day weeks, ten-hour days, weekends that are no different from weekdays, or canceled vacations.

That same Entrepreneurial Author *does* know what it's like to work twenty days in a row, to burn gallons of midnight oil, and to sacrifice a holiday for a work emergency. But these are exceptions to the rule. And the rule reminds you that *you are a human being first and a worker second.*

Who is in control of your destiny? *You are.* Once you understand the truth of that, you'll not veer down the road leading to becoming a workaholic, you'll know how to keep stress further away than arm's length, and you'll eventually become consciously addicted to a life with balance.

Hard work will benefit your business; overly hard work—in the form of draconian hours and days—will prevent you from operating at your sharpest. The Entrepreneurial Author sees clearly the line between working hard and working too hard. The Entrepreneurial Author uses the technologies of the day to save time without sacrificing quality or creating stress. If you experience stress, something is wrong and it must be diagnosed. Stress is a symptom of operational illness. Cure that illness with planning and commitment, and the stress will be alleviated.

Stress due to overwork has horrid side effects:

- It causes substantial increases in substance abuse, stress-related health problems, and the phenomenon of latchkey children left to fend for themselves and kids who feel as bonded to the day-care workers as they do to Mom and Dad.
- Half of all marriages will end in divorce.
- More than 60 percent of all kids born today will spend some time growing up in a single-parent family.
- The incidence of reported child abuse has quadrupled in the last decade, and spousal abuse is rising at an ugly rate.
- The average age of successful suicides is now forty. And there has been a 300 percent increase in the suicide rate for fifteen- to twenty-four-year-olds since the middle of the century, probably connected to single parenting.
- Cocaine and alcohol abuse actively touches six out of ten American families.
- The average working parent spends a mere *eleven minutes a day* of "quality time" with his or her children.

Entrepreneurial Authors ward off becoming workaholics by setting their projected finish times in advance, since people will work to fill up the allotted time. They set reasonable deadlines for themselves and make sure their customers or clients do the same. They prioritize their work, eliminating the nonsense. They are so aware of time that they don't even waste it, but always spend it wisely. They are keenly aware that work creates ruts and that after being formed, ruts will then trap them for the better part of a lifetime.

In the 1980s, working late was considered heroic and proper, a sign that the person was on her way to success. Work experts inform us that this attitude has shifted, that there has been a dramatic change in perception, and that mainstream thinking now holds that there is more to life than work. Says one time-management specialist: "I think the people who reject long hours will be the real leaders in the years to come—they're the brightest, the innovators. The guys logging really long hours aren't seen as heroes anymore. They're seen as turkeys."

The Great Sacrifice

When a person opts for becoming a workaholic, that person willingly sacrifices his own humanity for the almighty dollar. Or for status. Or power. Or because the workaholic is programmed like the worker ant—to toil without thinking, to set aside all sense of individuality.

The Entrepreneurial Author is very different from that fellow; the author is programmed to fulfill herself as a human being, to assert her individuality and nourish it, and to encourage it to bloom. We just didn't have the time for such reflection in the nine-to-five atmosphere of this past century. Our parents and grandparents set a pace that was ideal for them, but wrong for us, living as we do in an age brimming with leisure pursuits and the spiritual enlightenment to realize their importance.

The Good and Bad News

This age brings both good news and bad news. The good news is that along with the new millennium, we are entering a new world of work in which time and technology will take on new perspectives—in which people will actually take time to reflect upon their existence and work style.

The bad news is that not everyone is going to enter that new world. Some will be impeded by old notions and false perceptions. A lead article in *National Geographic,* which reported on the impact of information on the world, concluded with these words:

> Some of us will cross into the new world; others will remain behind. New worlders will pull even further ahead as technologies evolve … Technology promises more and more information for less and less effort. As we hear these promises,

we must balance faith in technology with faith in ourselves. Wisdom and insight often come not from keeping up-to-date or compiling facts but from quiet reflection. What we hold most valuable—things like morality and compassion—can be found only within us. While embracing the future, we can remain loyal to our unchanging humanity.

Workaholics, burnout, and stress were bugaboos of the bad old days. The Entrepreneurial Author lives in the present and wants it to be primarily made up of the good new days, so he makes the most of every precious moment and does not mortgage the present for the future.

TEN PITFALLS TO AVOID IN YOUR QUEST

You should know that there are more than ten pitfalls awaiting you on your journey to Entrepreneurial Authorship. Ten thousand is more like it. To avoid most of them, keep your eyes open and visualize the best while remembering that the worst is visualizing you. Entrepreneurial Authors are well acquainted with Murphy and his laws, consider him a wild-eyed optimist, and have learned to cross the street when they see him coming. You can avoid him too, merely by sidestepping the ten tempting entrepreneur traps. Wise men and women have been lured into them, never to escape.

An Entrepreneurial Author once said that she didn't want to be a passenger in her own life. That meant she had to assume the captaincy of her future and be in complete charge of all attainments and goof-offs, even fatal goof-offs. She had to learn to fend off temptation daily. Many authors are lured by "opportunities"—siren calls urging them to stray from their goals and wander off into someone's dream. Entrepreneurial Authors remain firmly committed to their own dreams.

All ten pitfalls listed here are traps you've probably foreseen anyway. The more you recognize them at the outset, the less likely you'll be to tumble into them when they're on your path. So take a few moments to peer down into them. The next time you see them, you can smile as you leap over them.

Pitfall #1: The Time Trap

As much as people revere leisure time, they have less of it than ever, averaging 32 percent less time than they had in the 1980s. Here I am jumping up and glorifying the three-day work week while increasing numbers of Americans are wondering how to get out from under the six-day workweek. Becoming an Entrepreneurial Author is the best way I know. But avoid doing all the work yourself, letting your ego get in the way of your dreams, failing to make the distinction between spending time and wasting time. If you find yourself spending too much time at the outset, you'll establish a pattern that will be very difficult to change later on. Habits are much easier to form than they are to break. "I'll just work sixty hours a week for now, and then I'll cut back later." It won't happen.

Pitfall #2: The Large Lure

While working my three-day work week and pulling in acceptable dollars, I used to wonder, but not very often, how much money I could make if I worked a six-day week. But the thought of giving up my four-day weekend was always too horrendous, and I lost little time entertaining that grandiose, stupid thought. More than a few times, clients have offered me alluring opportunities to do more for them for more money—which would have resulted in putting in more time. I accepted each opportunity, but with my proviso that I maintain the integrity of my work schedule. You'll be offered chances to earn more money, expand, take on more people, move to a larger space, and transform your business from an entrepreneurial endeavor to a large corporate entity. Hey, it's your life—but you've got to turn in your entrepreneurial credentials if you opt for size rather than freedom, for bigger rather than balance.

The Deepest Pit of All

Pitfall #3: The Money Morass

Said *Fortune* magazine, "Those driven solely by the desire for big bucks tend to be negligent of personal relationships.

The lack of time away from work for falling in love, sitting and talking with a spouse, or answering a child's question" contributes to the fact that mental health providers constitute a major growth industry. Money alters human behavior to the point that it causes well-meaning owners of small businesses bound for success to veer in the direction of financial success, steamrolling their chances for emotional, martial, parental, or social success. Money, which is easier to attain than balance, is more frequently sought. Those who pursue it find that the price they pay outstrips the money they gain. How do you put a price tag on a happy marriage or a well-adjusted kid anyhow? Of all the pitfalls, the Money Morass is the deepest, darkest, and biggest. If you fall into it, don't expect to find any fellow Entrepreneurial Authors at the bottom with you. They've learned that it is possible to earn a living without paying for it with their lives.

Pitfall #4: The Burnout Barrier

You'll search your soul to come up with a method for earning your livelihood, and you'll set up shop with all the right intentions. You'll work hard and smart, and your effort will bear fruit. But somewhere along the way, you might lose some of your initial enthusiasm for your work. You'll continue on because you've been successful, but you'll bring less and less joy to your work. The thrill will be gone. You'll have burned out.

If this happens to you, aim to *do something else.* You must make a change, large or small, to restore your enthusiasm—for without it, you're sunk. The trouble is, most business owners continue on without joy, not wanting to rock the boat that got them to their destination—even though that destination now means being lost at sea. They are bogged down by habit, by routine. If the spark is gone, get yourself another dream. Enthusiasm will fuel your fires, and if it is absent, the fire in your soul will go out—the fire that was key to your success. Entrepreneurial Authors know that they can relight the fire for a new venture, and studies irrevocably prove that the more you love what you do, the better you'll do it. So if you no longer feel the love, end the relationship and start another.

Pitfall #5: The Humanity Hindrance

I know I'm urging you to become an efficient earning machine, to realize the crucial importance of profits to a business, to work from home if you can, and to embrace technology as a means to your end. But I hope like crazy that you never lose your personal warmth, your sense of humor, or your love of other human beings in your quest to become a successful Entrepreneurial Author. Sadly, the world has more than enough tales of individuals who left a trail of shattered people on their climb to the top. The Entrepreneurial Author's priority list places people ahead of business, family ahead of business, love ahead of business, and self ahead of business. Keeping your eyes on the bottom line should not make them beady. Putting your heart in your work should not turn it to stone. Attaining everything on your wish list should not put you on anybody's enemy list. An executive I knew at a Fortune 500 company had a glass eye. When I asked which was the glass eye, I was told, "It's the warm one." No rule says that you must give up your humanity as the dues for achieving entrepreneurial success.

Growing Your Mind

Pitfall #6: The Focus Foil

Along the road to your goals, you'll find many sparkling roadside attractions beckoning you to stop for a while to linger. Linger you should, for investigation is the hallmark of The Entrepreneurial Author. But be certain to maintain focus on your goals while you're checking out the scenery. It is difficult to lose that focus and aim for a false goal, a tangential journey leading away from your dreams. You can become so involved in the details of your operation that you deviate from your primary thrust. Your time will become gobbled up by details instead of broad strokes. You can become wrapped up in a technology such as computer games, losing focus. You spend your time learning about your computer instead of broadening your business. Grow your mind as you grow your business, but maintain your direction—unless you consciously decide to make a change. I have nothing against a wholesale change, but if it is made by circumstance instead of by you, it's a major problem. Don't let your focus be foiled by anything except your own conscious intent.

Free from Imperfections and Perfectionists

Pitfall #7: The Perfection Pit

At the top of my own list of time-wasters, life-stealers, and company-ruiners are perfectionists and the pursuit of perfection. I am all for excellence and admire perfection in a bowling game or classroom attendance—two areas where perfection is possible. But how many drafts of a manuscript must a writer make? Does it become a perfect manuscript after the twentieth rewrite? I doubt it. Many authors become ensnared by their own high standards and the quest for elusive perfection. I am giddy with delight that the pilot who commands the jet carrying me to who-knows-where is a perfectionist. Same for the people who made the plane. But I don't recommend perfection as a goal unless public safety is at risk. Instead

I recommend it as a guide. Entrepreneurial Authors try to be perfect, but they don't spend all their time and energy attaining perfection. They spend their time polishing the unpolishable, steeped in the unnecessary, devoted to the unattainable. A perfect memo? A perfect direct mail letter? A perfect design scheme? Give me a break. May your enterprise be free from imperfections and from perfectionists.

Pitfall #8: *The Selling Snare*

The selling snare forces you to sell the same thing over and over again. The Entrepreneurial Author's way around it is to *make multiple sales with one effort*. Instead of a single issue magazine, sell a subscription. Rather than a single massage, sell a year's worth of weekly massages. Entrepreneurial Authors do all in their power to develop products or services that must be purchased on a regular basis. You work hard to close a sale. If you've got to get up and do it again and again, the bloom may soon fade from your entrepreneurial rose. But if you work just as hard and manage to close ten years' worth of sales, that bloom will enjoy a long period of radiance. Many offerings are sold with repeat sales built right in, from our own Guerrilla Marketing Association to cable television, from cleaning services to diaper services, from insurance coverage to gardening, from swimming pool maintenance to dental care. Apply the ultimate in selling skills so that your one-time sale can lead to years and years of profits. If you fall into the trap of selling single shots only, you'll be spending more time selling than enjoying the benefits of your efforts.

Pitfall #9: The Leisure Lure

Don't kid yourself into believing that leisure time is automatically a good thing. Leisure time, when you don't know what to do with it, can lead to a wide variety of problems—from boredom to substance abuse. Truth be told, many people actually enjoy their work time more than their leisure time because at least they know what they'll be doing with their work time—they haven't a clue about how to spend their leisure hours. Entrepreneurial Authors do have a clue. And a hobby. And a slew of interests beyond working and earning money. They enjoy their leisure almost as much as their work, because they've given a lot of thought to what they'll do with their free time. They know that free time by itself can be a drag.

Free Time Can Be a Drag

I have zero problems with free time and can always fill it. And occasionally I take immense pleasure at going to sleep knowing I have accomplished absolutely nothing that day. Goofing off is one of my leisure activities. Instead of a vice, in this competitive and entrepreneurial age, it's an Entrepreneurial Author's virtue.

Pitfall #10: The retirement Ruse

It's horrid but true: more than 75 percent of retirees die within two years of their retirement. When they retire from work, it's as though they also retire from life. Don't make the mistake of planning for retirement. Plan on cutting down, on easing off, but not on quitting altogether.

Working keeps you sharp and keeps your brain in shape. Ceasing to work allows your brain to atrophy. What are most retirees concerned with? Well, 38 percent say they don't have enough money. Another 29 percent say they're fearful of not staying healthy. Eight percent say they have too much time on their hands, and they're bored. And 8 percent figure they probably won't live long enough to enjoy life.

Entrepreneurial Authors have enough money because they put retirement into the same category as imprisonment. The money continues to flow into their lives long after their cohorts have retired. They stay healthy because continuing to hone the edge caused by work results in the maintenance of health and increased longevity. They do not suffer from the problem of having too much time, because they have just enough work—just enough for play. And they have been enjoying life all along because they've been engaged in the work they love, a trademark of The Entrepreneurial Author. In nature, nothing ever retires, and as we get closer to understanding our own relationship with nature, we are discovering that retirement is unhealthy and contraindicated in anyone with brain waves.

It's okay to retire from work just as long as you remain active in something else. Golf is okay. So is mastering the Internet. Walking in the woods qualifies as a worthwhile activity. And so do painting and photography. As an Entrepreneurial Author, you are your own boss. No one is to *make* you retire. If you are no longer interested in the work your business provides you, find a different job for yourself within your own company. That's the luxury of being your own boss and calling you own shots. But what happens if you are simply no longer interested in the business? My advice is to retire from it—then move on to another dream. If perfecting your golf game is your next dream, go for it. But just don't retire from life itself. The trap of planning for retirement is like planning your own slow suicide brought on by inactivity.

THE NEED FOR PASSION

What's more important to the success of a business than common sense, experience, and enlightenment? I'll bet you answered the question correctly with your first guess if your first guess was *passion*.

Reach down into yourself to measure your own passion about these aspects of your life:

1. *You feel passion toward your product or service.* If you don't feel it, it will be difficult to muster the enthusiasm that fuels consistent sales. Enthusiasm, like passion itself, is contagious. If you have it, your staff, publisher, customers,

and network members feel it as well. If you don't, your apathy will spread to those same people.

2. *You feel passion toward your readers.* You want them to get exactly what they need. Your understanding of them ensures that their needs and your offerings are an ideal match. You feel passionate about your ability to satisfy your customers. If you don't, they're going to sense it, and someone else's passion will woo them for you.

3. *You feel passion about your company.* You know how hard you work to do things right and to connect with people who will treat your customers like royalty. You have a vision for your company, and you know how to turn it into a glorious reality. Your passion keeps you focused on this vision and guides your behavior in running your business. Like basketball fans who say "I love this game!" in commercials, you frequently find yourself thinking, "I love this company!" If you aren't able to sincerely think that thought, make changes so that you can.

4. *You feel passion about your employees or network members.* As an Entrepreneurial Author, you hired or joined forces with these people because of their attitude, and you feel good chemistry in relation to them. You know how hard they've worked for you, how they give your goals such high priority, and how valuable they are to you. No wonder you

feel such passion. They return it by their commitment to your company and by being passionate themselves.

5. *You feel passion about your day-to-day work.* Don't just sit there and take such a bold statement for granted. A lot of people are doing work for which they felt passion once upon a time, but no longer. If that's you, get yourself another line of work—please. You don't want to hold back your company or fellow networkers because you no longer feel the thrill you once felt. Do something different for the company, or do entirely different work yourself. After all, we're talking about your life, and that gets top priority in the passion department.

6. *You feel passion about your marketing.* If you don't, be sure that someone in your company does. Ideally, you will feel strongly about it even if you're not the person creating it. After all, marketing does supply the power that makes your company grow, that produces profits, and that keeps the morale up. If you do not feel passion about creating your marketing, I hope you feel it for the marketing itself and especially for the results it brings about for your firm.

7. *You feel passion about your service.* You don't confine service to what's written in a policy, but instead know that great service is whatever the customer wants it to be. You are

passionate about giving that kind of service. After all, that's the kind of service you'd love to receive yourself. If you feel passion about rendering superlative service, your customers sense it and remember it. If you don't feel passion, they also sense it and remember it.

8. *You feel passion about improving.* You are not content to kick back and congratulate yourself on work well done. Instead you know that smart people are constantly trying to make your customers their customers, so you feel passion about being the best company in your community, industry, or both. As long as your service is of superb quality, you are not afraid of change—only of falling behind. Your passion for improvement keeps you the best.

9. *You feel passion about learning.* You know the importance of knowledge in the coming millennium and that the most powerful basic human instinct is to learn. As an Entrepreneurial Author, you feel passionate about becoming better informed, smarter, and more knowledgeable about everything connected with your company, as well as your life. The day you stop feeling passion about learning is the day you may be on the way to becoming illiterate. Alvin Toffler, the author of *Future Shock,* said, "The illiterate of the future will not be the person who cannot read. It will be the person who does not know how to learn." And famed UCLA basketball

coach John Wooden added, "It's what you learn after you know it all that counts." Will you ever reach a point when you think you know it all?

10. *You feel passion about being an Entrepreneurial Author.* That passion carries with it a devotion to a life of balance. It means you feel passionate about freedom and time, arranging your life so that you have enough of those precious gifts built into it to enjoy the fruits of your business. You are an author bound for success and enjoying the journey, but you are a human being first, who values more in life than financial gain and increased size.

The Entrepreneurial Author's Edge

Fortunately, as an Entrepreneurial Author, you've got an edge. This edge keeps the fires of your *passion* burning brightly. It gives you a decided advantage over the authors who preceded you, because it helps you avoid their mistakes and built upon their successes. It is, without question, the way of The Entrepreneurial Author.

You have The Entrepreneurial Author's edge in *insight*. You've given thought to your priorities. You aren't going to be misled by the entrepreneurial myths involving overwork, overgrowth, and overextending your reach. You realize that your journey is your destination and that your plan is your road map. This insight will help you maintain your passion.

You have The Entrepreneurial Author's edge in *relationships*. Every sale you make leads to a lasting relationship. Every reader you get is going to be a customer for life. Your sales and even profits will probably go up and down, but your number of relationships will constantly go up, and your sales and profits will eventually follow.

You have The Entrepreneurial Author's edge in *service*. You see your service from your customer's point of view, not merely from your own. You realize that your service gives you an enormous competitive advantage over those who may be larger but less devoted to making and keeping customers delighted with your business. You know well the power of word-of-mouth marketing and how it derives from excellent service.

You have The Entrepreneurial Author's edge in *flexibility*. You are not enslaved by policies and by precedent. Instead, you are fast on your feet, sensitive to customer needs, and aware that flexibility is a tool for building relationships, profits, and your overall business. You are guided by the situation at hand and not by the way things were done in the past. Your flexibility adds to the passion that others feel about your company.

You have The Entrepreneurial Author's edge in *follow-up*. You don't have to be reminded about the number of potential relationships that are destroyed when customers are ignored after they make a purchase. Rather than ignoring them, you pay attention to them, remind them of how glad you are that they're customers, and pepper them with special offers, inside information, and care.

They never feel ignored by you and reciprocate by never ignoring your business when it comes to repeat purchases or referrals.

You have The Entrepreneurial Author's edge in *cooperation.* You see other businesses as potential partners of yours, as firms that can help you as you help them. You don't keep your eyes peeled for competitors to annihilate, but for businesses to team up with to form networks. Your attitude will help you prosper in an era when people are forming small businesses in droves.

You have The Entrepreneurial Author's edge in *patience.* As an Entrepreneurial Author, you are not in a hurry and never in a rush. You know how important time is, but you also know how too much speed results in diminished quality. Because of your planning, you avoid emergencies and high-pressure situations. Patience is one of your staunchest allies.

You have The Entrepreneurial Author's edge in *economy.* You know how to market without investing a bundle of hard-earned money. You have learned that time and energy are valuable substitutes for large budgets. You realize that in most business activity, you have a choice of any two of these three factors: speed, economy, and quality. You always opt for economy and quality. Your patience helps you economize.

You have The Entrepreneurial Author's edge in *timeliness.* You run a streamlined operation, devoid of fluff or unnecessary work. Your comfort with technology allows you to operate at maximum effectiveness. Your business is a state-of-the-art enterprise because it operates in the environment of today rather than that of ten years ago. Although you focus on your plan, you know the magic of proper timing and can make adjustments so that you are available just when customers need you.

You have The Entrepreneurial Author's edge in *commitment*. This commitment will set you apart from many other authors. It will help you achieve your aims with confidence. It is so powerful that you feel passion toward the commitment, and the commitment to power your passion. Without this inner commitment, even the best plans may go awry. With it, plans turn into a bright reality.

The Radiant Light of Love

The closer you examine it, the more you see that the way of The Entrepreneurial Author is illuminated by the radiant light of *love*—love of self, work, family, others, freedom, independence, and life. The Entrepreneurial Author has a lifelong love affair with life. The deeper and more heartfelt her love, the more she is capable of generating the fiery and exquisite passion that fuels her business and ignites her entire life.

The Time Has Never Been Better

In the history of humankind, there has never been a better time to be an Entrepreneurial Author than right now. All the circumstances are now in your favor—the mindset, the technology, and the splintering of many large businesses into even more small businesses.

Throughout the world, others are embarking on the same path that you will tread. Many are authors, but few are Entrepreneurial Authors. Some will fail because the lure of largeness is too strong. Some will fade because they don't understand the role of balance in their lives.

But Entrepreneurial Authors will succeed.

They will not judge the future by the past. They will be able to place work in the proper perspective. They will feel a sense of continual excitement about what they do. And they will be well aware of their edge over others.

Their passion—the fire in their hearts—will serve as the ultimate edge.

CHAPTER 5

The Next Steps

As an author, you are an entrepreneur. Every book you write is a separate enterprise, a business with its own fate and its own reckoning that balances income against expenditures.

Why One Equals Four

Every business is four businesses:

- An enterprise that creates a product or service
- A marketing business that sells what it produces
- A service business that understands that service is whatever customers want it to be
- A people business that makes the first three possible

The larger the business, the harder it is to establish and maintain personal relationships with customers, suppliers, and employees. Although they may be poor in capital, guerrillas can be rich in human capital through their relationships with the people in their networks.

One advantage you have over big businesses is that you can establish and maintain warm personal relationships—online and offline—with your readers and other allies in your assault on the citadel of fame and fortune. In the age of multinational conglomerates, consumers appreciate more than ever relationships with businesses that provide them with impeccable service and personal involvement.

According to Amazon.com founder Jeff Bezos, one of Amazon's goals is to be the world's most "customer-centric" company. They want to establish relationships with customers that are so satisfying customers won't be tempted to start from scratch and build relationships with competitors. For an Entrepreneurial Author, being the world's most "reader-centric" writer is a worthy goal.

Although Entrepreneurial Authors are committed to the success of their businesses, they value people more than sales. They pursue their goals ethically, and whenever possible, by providing more than what they promise.

Six Tactics

Six tactics of thinking like an Entrepreneurial Author:

1. Think new. Try to come up with fresh ideas that haven't been done before. People like to try new things. New ideas can excite people more than ideas that have been done before, even if they were successful. If you and your networks can't

dream up something new, use your creativity to give old ideas a new twist.

2. Think inclusively. Create ways to bring people together in a way so enjoyable they will tell friends about it before and after the event.

3. Think big. Look at the promotional opportunities your books create with the same breadth of vision you use to look at your books in the largest possible way. Then pare your ideas down to what you can accomplish. Promotion, like politics, is the art of the possible.

4. Think ideas through. Balance the time and energy you need to execute ideas against the potential gain in sales and publicity.

5. Think of a way out. Set benchmarks in time and energy to see if you're making the progress you need to make an idea worth implementing. If in the course of trying to follow through on an idea, you become convinced that the payoff won't justify the effort, let it go and move on to the next idea.

6. Think of ways to be a giving enterprise, not just a taking one. Make a virtue of commerce by helping your community while you promote your book. Schools, libraries, and charities always welcome help raising funds. You will feel better about your efforts and so will others involved with

them. And the media is more likely to cover a charity event than a purely commercial one.

One reason now is such a great time to be a writer is that you can use the books you love and the authors you admire as models for creating your books and your career.

You can bring your vision, passion, and creativity to promotion—your unique ability to do the same things differently and better than they've been done before. One way to know you're succeeding: Other authors use your ideas.

The more skills and interests you have, the more possibilities they will create for promoting your books—so develop your skills, knowledge, and creativity as much as you can in as many fields as you can. They will serve you well.

The Entrepreneurial Author's Ten Commandments

How much it helps you and your books depends on how closely you follow this advice:

1. Create books, products, and services that you can market with pride and passion.

2. Remember that you are in the service of your ideas, your books, and your readers.

3. Establish an annual marketing budget that reflects your belief in the importance of marketing and enables you to carry out your promotion plan.

4. Devote the same time, energy, and imagination to promoting your books every day that you devoted to writing them.

5. Foster and sustain warm, giving relationships with your networks.

6. Maintain the perspective of a one-person multimedia, multinational conglomerate when you make decisions about writing and promoting your books.

7. Be a lifelong learner in your field and in learning to market your business so you remain competitive.

8. Use state-of-the-art techniques and technology to serve your readers better.

9. Recommend competitors' books if they will meet readers' needs in ways that yours don't.

10. Practice "co-opetition" by seeking ways to benefit from collaborating with your competitors.

Of course, give more than your readers expect, which is why I'm going to do the same with ten more commandments:

11. Always over-deliver with the content of your books, seminars, talks, etc.

12. Make your marketing efforts creative and consistent enough to position yourself as one of the top authors in your field.

13. Welcome change as an opportunity to find ideas and improve your business and your life.

14. Make selling your books to new readers the start of a lifelong relationship.

15. Encourage readers to contact you, and regard this as an opportunity to serve them, to help attract new readers through word of mouth, and to publicize everything you can offer them.

16. Welcome the chance to say thank you and reward those who help you.

17. Let your decisions reflect harmonious short- and long-term personal and professional goals that make you eager to get up in the morning.

18. Ask the people involved with your books and your business to help you keep these commandments.

19. Strive to create harmony between what you think, say, and do without crossing the line between being righteous and self-righteous.

20. Understand that marketing begins once you've made the sale and that a mind-numbing 68 percent of all business lost is due to apathy after the sale.

Add your own commandments to this list, and share them with us so we can add them to the list.

An Author's Guide to an Industry
on the Edge of Tomorrow

I firmly believe that book publishing, like any other business, needs to be shaken by a revolution from time to time. The five most momentous revolutions in the history of human communication are the invention of speech, the invention of writing, Gutenberg's invention of movable type in the fifteenth century, the creation of computers in the twentieth century, and the introduction of the entrepreneurial publishing model in the twenty-first century.

You are writing books, getting them published, and promoting them while publishing is in the throes of the most profound yet promising upheaval in its two-hundred-year history. Experts predict that business will change more in the next five years than it has in the last five hundred.

Now is an amazing time to be alive. Capitalism, competition, consolidation, technology, and the globalization of culture and commerce are accelerating the transformation of civilization.

We are on a wildly exhilarating ride into an impossible-to-predict future. Nobody's in charge of the vessel, and no one knows where it's going, so hang on tight and enjoy the ride.

Guerrilla Marketing for Writers

The battle begins before your book even hits the shelves, and you need every weapon to get ahead of the competition. Jay Levinson,

Rick Frishman, Michael Larsen, and David Hancock have written *Guerrilla Marketing for Writers,* which puts an entire arsenal at your disposal. Packed with proven insights and advice, it details 100 classified secrets that will help to sell your work before and after it's published. This wide range of weapons—practical low-cost and no-cost marketing techniques—will help you design a powerful strategy for strengthening your proposals, promoting your books, and maximizing your sales.

Get your copy today. With more than 20 million *Guerrilla* books sold in sixty-two languages, you'll be making the right choice.

{Claim Your Bonus}

The Entrepreneurial Author Community

Until now, no writers association in existence could make an author bulletproof. But once again, Jay Conrad Levinson, the most respected marketer in the world, and David Hancock, the father of The Entrepreneurial Author, have broken new ground. The Entrepreneurial Author Community is quite possibly a blueprint for author immortality.

Receive a two-month *free* trial membership in The Entrepreneurial Author Community, where guerrilla marketing coaches and leading business experts answer your business questions online and during exclusive weekly telephone chats and provide additional information, tips, tools, and techniques for your success as an Entrepreneurial Author.

This $99 value is your gift for investing in *The Entrepreneurial Author.*

Join right now—before your competition does—at:

Morgan-James.com/eac

{About the Author}
Jay Conrad Levinson

Jay Conrad Levinson is the author of the best-selling marketing series in history, "Guerrilla Marketing," plus 57 other business books. His books have sold 20 million copies worldwide. And his guerrilla concepts have influenced marketing so much that his books appear in 52 languages and are required reading in MBA programs worldwide.

Jay taught guerrilla marketing for 10 years at the extension division of the University of California in Berkeley. He was a practitioner of it in the United States—as Senior VP at J. Walter Thompson, and in Europe, as Creative Director of Leo Burnett Advertising.

A winner of first prizes in all the media, he has been part of the creative teams that made household names of many of the most famous brands in history: The Marlboro Man, The Pillsbury Doughboy, Charlie the Tuna, Morris the Cat,

Allstate's Good Hands, United's Friendly Skies, and the Sears Diehard Battery.

Jay is the Chairman of Guerrilla Marketing International. His Guerrilla Marketing is series of books, workshops, CDs, videos, a CD-ROM, a radio show, a University, a series of podcasts, an Internet landmark, and The Guerrilla Marketing Association—a support system for small business.

Guerrilla Marketing has revolutionized marketing because it is a way for business owners to spend less, get more, and achieve substantial profits. To transform you into a marketing guerrilla, there is no better person than The Father of Guerrilla Marketing— Jay Conrad Levinson.

JayView@aol.com
[415-453-2162]
www.GMarketing.com

Scan this 2D barcode with your
smart phone to access it's content.
(download a reader app to your phone:
get.beetagg.com)

{ABOUT THE AUTHOR}
David L. Hancock

David Hancock is a Certified Guerrilla Marketing Coach and the founder of Morgan James Publishing. Recognized in 2008 by NASDAQ as one of the world's most prestigious business leaders. He was also named a finalist in the Best Chairman category in the 2006 American Business Awards. Hailed as "the business world's own Oscars" by The New York Post, the American Business Awards are the only national, all-encompassing business awards program honoring great performances in the workplace.

David was selected for Fast Company magazine's Fast 50 for 2006 for his leadership, his creative thinking, his significant accomplishments, and his significant impact on the industry over the next ten years. David has revolutionized book publishing from the author's standpoint. His Entrepreneurial Publishing™ model enriches authors as well as the company.

David actively works with authors to help them not only maximize revenue from their book royalties, but also build new business and increase their revenue substantially through follow-on sales to their readers.

One of David's core values is having strong and mutually beneficial relationships. "We've spent years developing many of the key business relationships; that allows us to get our books in bookstores and the widespread Web coverage we've been able to achieve. We intend to stay constant in our pursuit of positive relationships with people in all facets of our business, and we see that as a strategic advantage."

David is the founder of the Entrepreneurial Author University and founder of the Ethan Awards, the only international, all-encompassing entrepreneurial author awards for business authors. David sits on the advisory board of the Mark Victor Hansen Foundation and on the executive board of Habitat for Humanity Peninsula. David has authored too many books to list them all here but they include The Entrepreneurial Author, Guerrilla Marketing for Writers, Guerrilla Marketing for Mortgage Brokers, The Secrets of Master Marketing, Affiliate Cash Flow Marketing and How to Join the eBay Game and Win.

David and his wife Susan live in Hampton Roads, Virginia, with their two children, Morgan Renee and Ethan James.

David can be reached at:

[516-522-0514]

DavidLHancock.com

Twitter.com/DavidHancock

FaceBook.com/DHancock

Scan this 2D barcode with your
smart phone to access it's content.
(download a reader app to your phone:
get.beetagg.com)

BUY A SHARE OF THE FUTURE IN YOUR COMMUNITY

These certificates make great holiday, graduation and birthday gifts that can be personalized with the recipient's name. The cost of one S.H.A.R.E. or one square foot is $54.17. The personalized certificate is suitable for framing and will state the number of shares purchased and the amount of each share, as well as the recipient's name. The home that you participate in "building" will last for many years and will continue to grow in value.

Here is a sample SHARE certificate:

YES, I WOULD LIKE TO HELP!

I support the work that Habitat for Humanity does and I want to be part of the excitement! As a donor, I will receive periodic updates on your construction activities but, more importantly, I know my gift will help a family in our community realize the dream of homeownership. **I would like to SHARE in your efforts against substandard housing in my community!** *(Please print below)*

PLEASE SEND ME _____ SHARES at $54.17 EACH = $ $_____

In Honor Of: _____

Occasion: (Circle One)   HOLIDAY   BIRTHDAY   ANNIVERSARY

OTHER: _____

Address of Recipient: _____

Gift From: _____ *Donor Address:* _____

Donor Email: _____

I AM ENCLOSING A CHECK FOR $ $_____ PAYABLE TO HABITAT FOR

HUMANITY <u>OR</u> **PLEASE CHARGE MY VISA OR MASTERCARD** *(CIRCLE ONE)*

Card Number _____ Expiration Date: _____

Name as it appears on Credit Card _____ Charge Amount $ _____

Signature _____

Billing Address _____

Telephone # Day _____ Eve _____

PLEASE NOTE: Your contribution is tax-deductible to the fullest extent allowed by law.
Habitat for Humanity • P.O. Box 1443 • Newport News, VA 23601 • 757-596-5553
www.HelpHabitatforHumanity.org

WITHDRAWN
BY
WILLIAMSBURG REGIONAL LIBRARY

LaVergne, TN USA
21 October 2009
161613LV00003B/2/P